PRACTICAL
BONSAI
PROJECTS

PRACTICAL

CREATE 23 SUPERB TREES

BONSAI

350 STEP-BY-STEP PHOTOGRAPHS

PROJECTS

All you need to learn about creating and displaying miniature trees and shrubs, shown in 23 detailed examples and illustrated with more than 350 colour photographs

Ken Norman

PHOTOGRAPHY BY NEIL SUTHERLAND

southwater

This book is dedicated to YOSHI, a lifelong best friend

This edition is published by Southwater

Southwater is an imprint of Anness Publishing Ltd
Hermes House, 88–89 Blackfriars Road, London SE1 8HA
tel. 020 7401 2077; fax 020 7633 9499

www.southwaterbooks.com; www.annesspublishing.com

If you like the images in this book and would like to investigate using them for
publishing, promotions or advertising, please visit our website
www.practicalpictures.com for more information.

UK agent: The Manning Partnership Ltd
tel. 01225 478444; fax 01225 478440; sales@manning-partnership.co.uk
UK distributor: Grantham Book Services Ltd
tel. 01476 541080; fax 01476 541061; orders@gbs.tbs-ltd.co.uk
North American agent/distributor: National Book Network
tel. 301 459 3366; fax 301 429 5746; www.nbnbooks.com
Australian agent/distributor: Pan Macmillan Australia
tel. 1300 135 113; fax 1300 135 103; customer.service@macmillan.com.au
New Zealand agent/distributor: David Bateman Ltd
tel. (09) 415 7664; fax (09) 415 8892

Publisher **Joanna Lorenz**
Senior Managing Editor **Conor Kilgallon**
Editors **Caroline Davison, Molly Perham and Liz Woodland**
Designer **Lisa Tai**
Editorial Reader **Rosie Fairhead**
Production Controller **Claire Rae**

Ethical Trading Policy
At Anness Publishing we believe that business should be conducted in an
ethical and ecologically sustainable way, with respect for the environment and a
proper regard to the replacement of the natural resources we employ.
As a publisher, we use a lot of wood pulp to make high-quality paper for
printing, and that wood commonly comes from spruce trees. We are therefore
currently growing more than 500,000 trees in two Scottish forest plantations near
Aberdeen – Berrymoss (130 hectares/320 acres) and West Touxhill (125
hectares/305 acres). The forests we manage contain twice the number of trees
employed each year in paper-making for our books.
Because of this ongoing ecological investment programme, you, as our
customer, can have the pleasure and reassurance of knowing that a tree is
being cultivated on your behalf to naturally replace the materials used to make
the book you are holding.
Our forestry programme is run in accordance with the UK Woodland Assurance
Scheme (UKWAS) and will be certified by the internationally recognized Forest
Stewardship Council (FSC). The FSC is a non-government organization dedicated
to promoting responsible management of the world's forests. Certification ensures
forests are managed in an environmentally sustainable and socially responsible
way. For further information about this scheme, go to
www.annesspublishing.com/trees

Previously published as part of a larger volume, *Growing Bonsai:
A Practical Encyclopedia*

Front cover main image: Japanese white pine (*Pinus parviflora*)
Page 1: *Juniper horizontalis* 'Green Carpet'
Page 2: Japanese maple (*Acer palmatum*)
Page 3: Chinese juniper (*Juniperus chinensis*)
Page 4, from top: Mountain pine (*Pinus mugo*); *Rhododendron
racemosum* 'Ginny Gee'; *Rhododendron* hybrid
Page 5, from top: Bird plum cherry (*Sageretia theezans*); *Acer palmatum* 'Nomura';
Three-lobed or Trident maple (*Acer buergerianum*)

Contents

Introduction

The Japanese word "bonsai" basically means a plant, tree, or group of trees or plants growing in a container (from *bon* "basin" and *sai* "to plant"). Bonsai is all about growing miniature trees in the form of full-size mature trees, mostly using the same species and varieties from which the full-size trees are grown. Bonsai is a fascinating living art form that can lead to a lifetime of studying and understanding trees – a study of full-size trees growing naturally can help you understand the various bonsai styles. It is not a hobby for those who demand quick results, but watching your bonsai develop from year to year, while perfecting your skills in training and caring for them, is hugely rewarding.

Above: Acer palmatum *'Ukon', styled into a beautiful twin-trunk bonsai is a typical example of a Japanese maple, but in miniature.*

WHERE TO START

Acquiring a ready-grown bonsai is how most people enter the world of bonsai as a hobby, and for many it then develops into an obsession. If you join a bonsai society you will find plenty of inspiration, as well as useful advice from experienced growers.

SUITABLE TREES AND SHRUBS

Pine, juniper, larch and cedar are some of the most popular coniferous trees that are turned into bonsai, and there are, of course, many more species from which to choose. Remember that larch is a deciduous conifer and will lose its foliage (needles) in the winter.

There are also a wide variety of deciduous trees to choose from, such as maple, elm, beech, hawthorn, hornbeam, Judas tree, pomegranate, crab apple, wisteria and many more. The last three also bear flowers and fruit, and it should be noted that flowers and fruit produced will always be their natural size even when a tree is grown and trained as bonsai.

When deciding which type of plant material to use, a visit to a good garden centre or plant nursery will probably be the best place to start. Look for a plant that exhibits a woody trunk structure with a reasonably chunky appearance. This will give you a head start when shaping your tree, as you will have something with a semi-mature appearance right from the start.

If you want a flowering bonsai, some of the most spectacular examples can be grown using rhododendrons and azaleas, of which there are a wide variety available.

Left: *Japanese maples* (Acer palmatum*) are some of the most popular plants from which bonsai specimens are created.*

Above: *Three bonsai, from left to right:* mame elm, shohin *juniper and* chumono *hornbeam. The three different sizes are shown here.*

INDOORS OR OUTDOORS?

If you wish to grow a tropical species as a bonsai in a temperate climate, you will need to keep it indoors for at least part of the year. Similarly, trees from temperate regions may need to be kept indoors if they are grown in a tropical or sub-tropical area.

BONSAI SIZES

A bonsai can be virtually any size as long as it is a potted plant that takes on the appearance of a full-size, mature specimen tree. To create the best effect, the pot and tree should complement each other, so much so that whatever their size they always take on an air of extreme maturity and elegance. You might expect that the smaller the bonsai the easier it is to look after, but in fact, the very small trees can be quite difficult to style and maintain.

PROPORTIONS AND AESTHETICS

The relationship between the overall height, width and depth of a bonsai is extremely important, just as the relationship between the density of foliage and thickness and taper of the trunk must be complementary. The thickness of the base of the trunk compared with the size and shape of the pot is equally crucial, and when all these elements are combined and related to each other a truly magnificent bonsai can be the result. Features such as the position of the first branch and whether it is on the left or right of the trunk can make or break the final appearance of your bonsai, so consideration of all these aspects is of the utmost importance.

BONSAI EQUIPMENT

There is a wide range of specialist bonsai tools designed for specific purposes when growing bonsai, but a few very basic gardening tools will suffice at the beginning of your bonsai career. As you become more experienced, however, you will find that specialist Japanese tools will start to appeal to you more. Given the ability and experience, it is possible to make some tools inexpensively, and general everyday tools can sometimes make a good substitute for the more expensive specialist ones. However you begin, you may well find it useful to keep your bonsai tools separate from any other gardening tools, as well as keeping them in a special tool container. You will also find it easier to work on your bonsai if you invest in a special turntable to stand them on.

Left: *A 44-year-old Japanese larch (*Larix kaempferi*) measuring 30cm (12in) in height.*

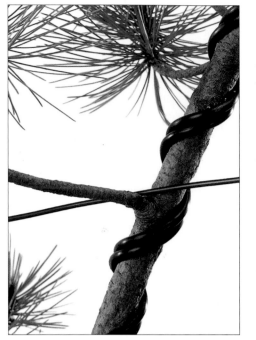

TOOLS FOR PRUNING

For small-scale pruning, involving trimming shoots and leaves, the most useful tool is a pair of pointed scissors. Normal secateurs (pruners) can be used for pruning branches, but they will leave a short stub. This will not only appear unsightly, but will also leave a wound that may never heal correctly. To carry out a much better, cleaner job, therefore, you should purchase some bonsai side or branch cutters. Using these cutters will enable you to make a clean concave cut close to the trunk, which results in a more rapid healing of the wound and so gives a much cleaner appearance to the tree. These cutters have a single curve to the cutting edges.

Possibly the next most useful tool to buy for your collection is a pair of "wen" or "knob cutters". These are mostly used to remove a branch or a branch stub close to the trunk. They have concave cutting edges in both directions, resulting in a small concave hollow that will heal much more quickly. By leaving such a hollow, you will help the callusing bark to "roll" into the hollow and leave only a slight trace of the pruning cut.

All cutting tools should be kept sharp and clean, to reduce the risk of introducing disease into a wound.

Left: *Wire can be used to shape your bonsai as well as pruning.*

TOOLS FOR WIRING

Wiring is an important part of the shaping process and requires a number of tools. The three main items normally used during the process of wiring a bonsai are wire cutters, pliers and the wire itself.

Wire cutters are available in several sizes, normally small, medium and large, but they can be very expensive if you buy the genuine Japanese article. You can, however, execute just as good a job with a standard pair of electrician's wire cutters, which can be purchased at a much lower price. The Japanese wire cutters are superior because they have longer handles in proportion to the cutting blades, which makes the process of cutting through thicker wires much easier than with the electrician's version. They also enable you to cut the wire close to the trunk or branch of the tree without damaging the bark.

A good pair of pliers can also be a very useful part of the wiring toolkit. Normally these would be the Japanese variety, called jinning pliers, which double up here for holding and bending thicker gauges of wire. These specialist pliers are normally used for the forming of jin (areas of removed bark, revealing heartwood below), but they can also be a very valuable asset as

a general-purpose bonsai item to add to your bonsai toolkit. Jinning pliers are useful for manipulating the "tying-in" wires when repotting. Once again, a more economical alternative to the Japanese pliers would be a standard pair of engineer's pliers.

Traditionally, annealed copper wire, which needs to be heated to soften (or anneal) each time it is reused, is used in the styling process. The special appeal of copper is that it oxidizes quickly and turns green, so that it blends with the bark of a tree to become inconspicuous. In recent years, however, anodized aluminium wire has become more popular because it is easy to use and can be reused without being heated. Nowadays, only more experienced growers use copper.

The wire is available in many gauges, from 1mm (1/25in) up to 6mm (1/4in) in diameter, and in rolls weighing 500g–1kg (1lb 2oz–2lb 4oz). The gauge of wire used must be thick enough to enable the branch or trunk to be held in place after it has been bent into shape.

SOILS FOR BONSAI

A good general-purpose soil mix is one part sphagnum moss peat, one part loam and two parts coarse sharp grit. The grit should have angular particles measuring 3–6mm (1/8–1/4in), but the edges should not be too sharp, as they

Above: *This shows the correct use of branch or side cutters, with the cutting edges held horizontally to the trunk.*

Above: *You can prune the roots of your bonsai plants with vine pruners or with ordinary household scissors.*

Above: *You will need to use wiring techniques when styling some bonsai plants. If this is the case, it can be easier to have a special dispenser containing wires of different gauges.*

Above: *Akadama is a good general-purpose bonsai soil. It should be dry when you pot up or repot your bonsai, to ensure good contact with the roots.*

can damage roots during repotting. Mix the ingredients when completely dry, and sieve them to obtain particles measuring 3–6mm (⅛–¼in), removing the fine dust so that the soil will be well aerated. The soil should also be dry when you pot your bonsai, as it will flow more easily around the roots.

Special bonsai soils from Japan are also available: akadama, a general-purpose clay granule soil; kanuma, for acid-lovers such as azaleas; and kiryu, especially suitable for pines and junipers.

WHERE TO GROW BONSAI

Trees that are hardy outdoors are best kept outside all year round – if protected in winter, they may be more susceptible to frost damage when the protection is removed.

Indoor bonsai need plenty of light, but not strong, hot sunlight. They also need more humidity than is usually present in centrally-heated homes – the easiest solution is to place them on a tray of absorbent granules, kept constantly moist (but make sure the water level is below the bottom of the pot).

Right: *You may find it easier to work on a specialist turntable when styling and caring for your bonsai.*

WATERING AND FEEDING

Since bonsai are deliberately kept in small pots to restrict their roots, they need frequent watering and feeding. Those kept outside may benefit from rain, but a thick leaf canopy may prevent it reaching the soil, and wind and sun can also mean they lose water very quickly.

The easiest way to water a bonsai, if the container is small enough, is to submerge the container completely in a bowl of water until the bubbles cease to rise, then remove and allow it to

drain. For larger containers, or if it is inconvenient to move them, use a watering can with a fine rose. You can also water or spray the foliage weekly. In winter, deciduous trees need less water – keep the soil slightly moist.

You can feed your plants with special slow-release bonsai fertilizer, or with a half-strength general-purpose liquid feed during the growing season. A specialist autumn fertilizer that contains no nitrogen will help to harden off the growth produced during the summer.

BONSAI STYLES

Styles of bonsai range from single-trunk designs through multiple-trunk to group and forest plantings. The style you decide upon will, to some extent, depend on the plant specimen you have chosen. Indeed, each tree will suggest a particular style, and you should follow that natural suggestion to obtain the best result.

One of the most important points to remember is that all styles of bonsai are based on the way trees grow in the wild. A natural-looking design is therefore the real test of a good bonsai, rather than how well it fits into any particular bonsai category. By observing full-size trees, you can soon start to appreciate how trees grow and into which styles your bonsai may fit.

When styling any tree, the first feature to look for is a good surface-root system. This will give the base of the trunk a more mature look. Rake the soil away from the trunk, exposing the roots to enhance the look of the trunk-to-soil junction.

All bonsai have a best angle, which is usually referred to as the front of the tree, but ideally every bonsai should look good from all angles.

Left: *Pruning a Chinese juniper* (Juniperus chinensis) *using bonsai scissors. Care must be taken to cut only the shoots and not the foliage.*

Formal Upright – *CHOKKAN*

The name of this style is self-explanatory, being upright, straight and very rigid and formal in appearance, a shape that occurs frequently in nature when a tree is growing in ideal conditions. This means that there are no severe or adverse weather conditions and a constant source of suitable nutrients, as well as a good sustainable supply of water. In this bonsai style, the trunk of the tree should ideally have a very even taper from soil level right up to the apex. This straightness and taper create a very elegant and statuesque design which is not apparent in any other style of bonsai. Although these trees can have a symmetrical appearance, this is not so in every case, as a certain amount of asymmetry will give a much more pleasing and natural look.

Above: This Cedrus libani *subsp.* atlantica *'Glauca' is typical of the plant material that is available from garden centres or nurseries and is approximately 1.2m (4ft) high.*

The tree's final shape should be well balanced and centred on the formal, vertical emphasis of the trunk. The branches will be mostly horizontal, which will help to accentuate the formal appearance of the trunk.

Suitable plants for styling as formal upright bonsai include many coniferous species such as pine (*Pinus*), larch (*Larix*), spruce (*Picea*) and juniper (*Juniperus*). Trees that normally develop an informal habit, such as fruiting and flowering varieties, are not very suitable for this style.

If the trunk is not completely straight, apply a piece of wire of suitable thickness and manipulate the trunk until it is straight when viewed from the front. Viewed from the side, the trunk should be angled very slightly to the rear as it rises from the soil, and again very slightly to the front in the upper part of the tree, giving the overall appearance of being vertical.

Assess which branches are best suited for the design. Choose a thick branch as the lowest one and then cut out any insignificant shoots, leaving

enough branches to complete the design. Apply wire to the branch, then, after running the wire around the trunk once or twice, wind it along the next branch up the trunk. Continue to wire the rest of the branches and arrange them so that they all complement each other. Finally, trim back the tips of the branches to give a balanced tree.

You will need
- Branch cutters
- Vine pruners
- Wire cutters
- Pliers
- Rake
- Pot
- Mesh
- Wire
- Soil
- Scoop
- Chopstick

CREATING YOUR FORMAL UPRIGHT BONSAI

1 Remove the top of the plant, leaving the thickest part of the trunk, which will give the future bonsai more "character".

2 Using a pair of branch cutters at an angle, remove the top of the plant to leave a tapered top to the trunk.

3 Following the removal of the top of the plant, it can be seen that the plant is beginning to show much better proportions as a future bonsai.

4 After the removal of one right-hand branch, a second similar branch is reduced in length, by approximately one-half, using side cutters.

5 This view shows how different the plant looks at this stage when compared with the first step of the sequence.

6 There are now too many minor branches still in place which will need pruning out using side or branch cutters.

7 One small branch has been removed, but there are still three more that must be cut off to give the plant a more open feeling.

8 There is still a long branch high up on the trunk that needs to be removed in order to give a better overall appearance to the tree.

9 This picture shows the plant after pruning, wiring and basic shaping has been completed, prior to being repotted into a suitable bonsai pot.

Right: *This is the completed tree, planted in a suitable pot and now ready for many years as a bonsai.*

Informal Upright – *MOYOGI*

This style is probably the most commonly seen style both in the natural environment and in bonsai. In the wild, an informal upright tree will have a trunk that bends and curves, and has changes of direction due to competition from other trees or buildings situated close by. These changes could be linked to the prevailing weather conditions surrounding the tree through the seasons. This is probably one of the easiest of bonsai styles to create, which makes it ideal for beginners. Many trees grow naturally with slightly bending or informal trunks, and you will find that working with these natural curves can create a pleasant bonsai design. Remember that any branches should appear to grow from the outside of a trunk curve in order to give a natural look to the finished tree.

Above: *A* Pinus sylvestris *'Jeremy' plant should be easily obtainable from a conifer nursery or garden centre.*

The trunk of an informal upright bonsai should be upright, but not absolutely straight, standing somewhere between the vertical and an angle of 15 degrees to the vertical. It should flow gently from one side to the other with a graceful, fluid form.

Examine the base of the trunk closely before carrying out any work. Carefully study the tree and try to decide on a preferred best side or front. It may be that it would be better viewed from a totally different angle to the one from which it has been seen in its original pot. Any curvature in the lower trunk as it rises from the soil should go in the rearward direction, as any forward bulge tends to look ugly. The trunk may then undulate from side to side and from front to back, finally finishing with the apex just forward of the trunk base. The branch structure is then designed around this informality, with branches coming from irregular points on the trunk and alternating from side to side and around the back. The front of the trunk should not have any branches pointing straight at the viewer unless they are small and near the top of the tree, where they become part of the crown. The informality of this design means that it is possible to style an informal upright bonsai using only pruning techniques and no wire at all.

CREATING YOUR INFORMAL UPRIGHT BONSAI

You will need
- Rake
- Scissors
- Branch cutters
- Tweezers
- Wire cutters
- Pliers
- Wound sealer
- Pot
- Mesh
- Wire
- Soil
- Scoop
- Chopstick

1 Use a rake to clear excess soil from the top of the root-ball until the roots can be seen growing from the lower trunk.

2 Loose surface roots exposed by the raking process can now be identified and the "flare" of the trunk base can now be clearly seen.

3 Remove loose roots with sharp scissors, leaving a soil surface that shows a clean trunk base and some thicker surface roots which will become features in the future.

4 Using branch cutters, remove the central upward-pointing branch in order to open up the structure of the tree.

5 This is the central shoot following removal with a pair of branch cutters.

6 All excess branches should be eliminated until a basic tree shape begins to emerge.

7 Using a pair of tweezers, pull out the old, dark, stiff needles on the trunk and main branches, leaving only those on the shoot ends.

▷

8 You can also remove the needles by gently pulling them out with your fingers.

9 The amount of needles remaining can be clearly seen and the tree is now ready for shaping by wiring and tip pruning.

10 Wind the wire around the trunk and branches at an angle of about 45°, looping it back on itself at the end of each branch.

11 The tree is now fully wired and ready for careful manipulation into shape using gentle bending so that you do not break any of the branches.

12 The wire can be applied to two branches and anchored to the trunk between the two branches.

13 This detail of the lower right branch clearly shows how the branch has been bent into a zigzag shape which will eventually enhance the appearance of the tree by giving it greater maturity.

14 The shaping is finished and the tree is now ready to be planted into a suitable bonsai container.

Right: *A Japanese white pine (*Prunus parviflora*), after many years of bonsai training.*

Slanting - *SHAKAN*

This bonsai style is based on a tree growing in the wild that has been exposed to strong winds and very stormy weather, so that it has blown over at an angle slanting away from the prevailing wind. The natural reaction of the tree after this has happened is to redirect its branch growth to suit the new growing angle of the trunk. Most species of tree can be grown in this style and examples in nature can be seen on cliff tops and in mountainous areas where there is a prevailing wind that pushes the tree over to one side. When this becomes more pronounced, it generally falls into the windswept category, but it is difficult to draw a distinction between these two styles.

The slanting style of bonsai should have its trunk leaning to one side, usually by about 45 degrees from the vertical, although it can be as much as 60 degrees. The trunk need not necessarily be straight – it can have some movement in its shape – but the apex should always take on the same angle as the one formed where the trunk rises from the soil.

Following the slant of the trunk, the roots will normally be extended on the side away from the slant, while those on the side under the slant will be compressed. This gives the impression of the roots stabilizing what would otherwise be an unstable-looking design.

The basic steps described previously to ascertain the trunk angle and root structure should be followed so that the angle of the trunk looks as natural as possible. The position of the branches must relate to the trunk so that a mature shape is obtained. Should a branch need to be placed in a drooping position, ensure the junction with the trunk bends down as soon as it leaves the trunk to achieve a natural effect.

Above: *This is a hybrid* Rhododendron *that is commercially available from any good supplier of this type of material and measures 65cm (26in) from the top of the pot to the apex.*

When you are styling a bonsai from scratch, make sure that all of the branches are properly positioned, including the smallest twigs. The degree of attention to this type of detail in the early stages of styling can make or break the appearance of the end product. A suitable type of pot can be seen in the final picture.

CREATING YOUR SLANTING BONSAI

You will need
- Stiff brush
- Branch cutters
- Wound sealer
- Scissors
- Wire cutters
- Pliers
- Rake
- Pot
- Mesh
- Wire
- Soil
- Scoop
- Chopstick

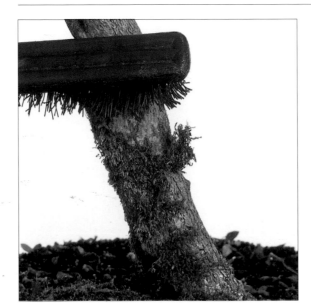

1 The moss that has grown on the lower part of the trunk of the *Rhododendron* should be removed using a stiff brush, so that the plant has a completely clean trunk. The soil of bonsai trees is always just moist and this provides the ideal conditions in which moss will grow. The lower parts of the trunks can quickly become covered in moss, which should be removed regularly.

2 The lower part of the tree trunk has now been completely cleared of unwanted moss and the beautiful texture and colour of the bark can be clearly seen.

3 There are two branches growing from the same point on the trunk, one of which must be removed in order to improve the tree's structure. Using branch or side cutters, remove the branch with a clean cut close to the main trunk.

4 Following the removal of the excess branches and some thinning out of the twigs and foliage in the upper part of the plant, the shape is now much improved. This tree has a long way to go before it becomes properly shaped with an aged-looking branch structure. Several years of shoot pinching, refinement, repotting and correct feeding will produce an excellent flowering bonsai.

Right: *The tree is planted in a temporary pot because it is not known, at this stage, exactly what colour, shape or design of pot should be chosen. When the bonsai specimen is finally developed, it may need a slightly different glazed or semi-glazed pot for display purposes.*

Semi-cascade – *HAN-KENGAI*

This style reflects the effect of extreme growing conditions on a tree. It is designed to give the appearance of a very old tree growing from the side of a quarry or rock face, or perhaps on a riverbank, where all the tree's efforts have gone into growing towards the light. Although the trunk line may initially have been upright, in natural conditions it could have been bent over into a nearly horizontal position by falling rocks, stones or soil. Ideal material for training as semi-cascade bonsai are prostrate-growing plants, such as cotoneaster and juniper, which can be bought from plant nurseries.

Semi-cascade is the name that is usually given when a bonsai leans over to one side or the other from 45 to 60 degrees from the vertical, even as low as just below the horizontal or the rim of the pot. Some people think that it should not go below the rim, while others think that going just below this point often gives a better and more appealing appearance.

Most types of tree can be grown in the semi-cascade style, except for those that normally have a very powerful vertical growth habit which will overcome the forces of nature. It is important to note that if a tree leans so far that it droops over the edge of the pot and down the side, it should then be classed as cascade-style bonsai.

Just as with the slanting style, there needs to be some root exposure in order to give the feeling of a stabilizing structure at the base of the trunk. Following the initial steps for the formal upright and informal upright bonsai styles that we have already described, assess the structure of the

Above: *The widely available creeping juniper,* Juniperus horizontalis *'Green Carpet', is ideal material from which a semi-cascade bonsai can be developed.*

roots, as well as the line of the trunk. Work with the natural flow of the tree, if possible accentuating any of those natural features.

A suitable container would be square, hexagonal or any other regular shape, and it should be of a medium depth so that it is in balance with the tree.

You will need
- Branch cutters
- Wound sealer
- Scissors
- Rake
- Pot
- Mesh
- Wire
- Wire cutters
- Pliers
- Soil
- Scoop
- Chopstick

CREATING YOUR SEMI-CASCADE BONSAI

1 Remove the plant from the original plastic pot and remove any adventitious foliage to expose a clean trunk base. This will provide a better insight into the styling possibilities of this particular plant.

2 Remove the left-hand branch, using a pair of branch or side cutters in order to obtain a clean concave cut.

3 The plant is now ready to be planted into a bonsai container, following the removal of all the excess twigs and foliage.

4 After repotting into a suitable container, the tree is now in the early stages of becoming a fully styled bonsai specimen.

Below: *The finished styling exercise is shown here displayed on a flat slab of sandstone. This shows the basic shape following initial styling. With regular shoot pinching, the foliage area will bulk up over the next few growing seasons.*

Cascade – *KENGAI*

Once again, this style of bonsai represents a tree that has been growing in very difficult circumstances, such as out of the side of a rock face or somewhere similar. In fact, this style is intended to represent a tree in the wild that has been subjected to heavy winter snowfall, rock falls, avalanches and, indeed, its own weight, all of which would cause it to lean and fall vertically from wherever it is rooted. This particular design can be obtained by repositioning various parts of the trunk line and branches, so that a cascading and mature outline is achieved.

In this style, the trunk line will fall well below the horizontal, with its trunk tip resting level with the bottom of the pot or even lower. Just as with the semi-cascade style, the trunk line generally begins by growing almost vertically from soil level before cascading over and down the side of the pot.

This style is not easy to produce and would normally be considered an advanced project if one wished to achieve a satisfying result. A suitable plant to use would be one that has a long, flexible trunk that can be easily manipulated with wire into an interesting cascade design. Such a plant need not already be cascading at the time of acquisition – it can be vertical or any other shape – but it is essential that the trunk is long and flexible.

All the usual initial procedures should be followed, such as looking at the base of the trunk and the formation of the roots, before deciding on the best way forward. Be careful when applying wire and with the subsequent bending because there is a

Above: *This is a typical, young* Cotoneaster horizontalis *that, due to a flexibility, is highly suited for styling as a cascade bonsai.*

risk of breaking the trunk. Should this happen, however, you could always use the tree for a totally different style.

Cascade bonsai require relatively deep pots to show off the cascading characteristics that you have designed. The pot shape should be regular but can, in some circumstances, also be natural and primitive in appearance to match the rugged look of the tree.

CREATING YOUR CASCADE BONSAI

You will need
- Branch cutters
- Scissors
- Wire cutters
- Pliers
- Wire
- Rake
- Pot
- Mesh
- Soil
- Scoop
- Chopstick

1 When working on a cascade bonsai, it may be helpful to work with the plant positioned on its display stand or post. The first part of the trunk should be cleared of growth, so remove any unwanted material in this area.

2 Begin wiring the trunk by pushing the end of the wire deep into the soil for anchorage.

3 Carefully wind the wire around the trunk to the length that is required, and cut the wire ends cleanly when the process is complete.

4 If the trunk is extra thick, a second run of wire may be needed which can be applied alongside the first. This gives twice the bending power of one run of wire.

5 Using both hands, and your thumbs as levering points, carefully shape the trunk until a full cascading effect is achieved.

6 Continue the process further along the trunk until the whole of the trunk has been shaped satisfactorily.

7 Remove the excess growth, once you have decided on the final length of the trunk.

8 Here, the leading shoot is being removed in order to balance the length of the trunk.

9 Following the full wiring of the trunk and side branches, the tree is now ready to be placed in a decorative bonsai pot.

Right: *The styling is now complete and the bonsai has been potted in a Chinese pot and displayed on a late 19th-century plant stand. A tall stand enables the tree to be seen in the correct perspective.*

Twin Trunk – *SOKAN*

The twin-trunk style is a very popular arrangement of two trees. This occurs naturally when a tree grows with two trunks from ground level. A twin trunk such as this may be the result of seeds germinating close together. As the two plants grow, they combine by natural grafting into one joined at the base. A bonsai twin-trunk tree can be created either by planting two or more trees very closely together or by starting with a plant that already has two or more trunks. If you are starting with a plant that has more than two trunks, then clearly any other trunks will need to be removed. The choice of which trunks to remove depends upon the shape and position of all the trunks on the plant. You will need to select the best pair of trunks in terms of their relationship with each other to achieve a balanced final appearance.

Above: *'Ginny Gee' is a* Rhododendron racemosum *hybrid and is ideal for bonsai by virtue of its small leaves and flowers.*

The simplest way to begin is to buy a twin-stemmed plant from a nursery and convert it into bonsai following the steps shown here. If, however, you have two trees from which to work, tie them tightly at the base with raffia or grafting tape so that they graft together at this point as they grow. Avoid tying with wire, as this has no flexibility and can create a rather unsightly union, especially with smooth-bark species. Check the junction regularly during the early part of the process to ensure that it is going according to plan.

If there had been a space between the two plants in the early years of growth, the expansion of the trunk girths would have been so large that a natural twin-trunk specimen would be the end result.

Always use two plants of the same variety, so that the leaf shape and colour are the same. Also ensure that the two plants have different-sized trunks: the main trunk should be taller with a larger girth than the other trunk. If the two trunks are identical in girth, or almost identical, then the

bonsai will look too regimented. If you want to find a suitable twin-trunk tree in the wild, then remember to look for one with unequal-sized trunks.

When considering the viewing angle of this style, arrange the smaller trunk so that it is alongside the main trunk, but slightly to the rear or to the front of it, as this will give a much better appearance.

CREATING YOUR TWIN TRUNK BONSAI

You will need
- Rake
- Branch cutters
- Scissors
- Pot
- Mesh
- Wire cutters
- Pliers
- Wire
- Soil
- Scoop
- Chopstick

1 After removing the plant from its pot, gently rake away the surface of the soil until the base of the trunk and any surface roots begin to show, and cut out any excess lower shoots until a clear tree image is formed.

Right: *Following pruning and styling, the tree has been planted in a deep rectangular pot and displayed on a simple oak stand. Compared with the off-centre placing on the stand in the picture above, it can be seen that a central placing is best.*

2 Clear away any excess internal shoots and minor branches until the required shape emerges.

3 The finished tree after the pruning and styling process has been completed.

Triple Trunk – *SAMBON-YOSE*

Multiple plantings should consist of three, five, seven and so on as a well-balanced group is difficult to achieve with even numbers except two. Here, we will be looking at the approach to a triple-trunk planting that can often be seen growing naturally in the wild. Any species of tree may be used to create this style of bonsai, but you will discover that it is largely conifers that have this type of growth formation. The plant material that you choose will need to include three plants with trunks of varying thicknesses, as well as of different heights. However, bear in mind that the heights of the trunks can be altered easily by pruning. Trees that have one-sided root systems would also be highly suitable because the bases of the trunks will need to be placed very closely together to create a satisfactory final design.

Above: *Three European larch plants,* Larix decidua, *in plastic flowerpots, which can be purchased from nurseries or garden centres.*

The trees chosen for this grouping are European larch (*Larix decidua*), and have been growing in individual pots for several years. They are about 20 years old and have trunks of varying thickness, which is very important when you are putting a group of this type together.

The traditional approach is to select the tree with the thickest trunk as the main tree which should then be placed towards the front of the grouping, with the subsequent positioning of the other two trees also being extremely important. Each tree must be securely attached to the pot and to the bases of the other two trees in order to encourage them to grow even more closely together as they mature alongside each other.

When cutting the roots back to enable the trees to be placed close together, it must be remembered that sufficient roots need to remain on each tree to enable them to survive the process and to grow on in the future. When the roots have been cleaned of soil, it is also necessary to keep the roots moist to prevent the trees from suffering dehydration. Use a fine atomizing spray to apply a fine mist of water to the roots if they appear to be drying out.

Once the trees are secured and the soil topped up and watered, the branches will need to be wired and manipulated into place to give the trees a mature overall design.

You will need
- Pot
- Mesh
- Wire
- Soil
- Wire cutters
- Branch cutters
- Scissors
- Pliers
- Rake
- Scoop
- Chopstick

CREATING YOUR TRIPLE TRUNK BONSAI

1 Prepare the bottom of the initial training pot with "butterfly" mesh retainers and "tying-in" wire.

2 This is the inside of the training pot showing the drainage mesh and "tying-in" wires in place.

3 Place a layer of coarse akadama over the bottom of the pot in order to improve drainage, followed by some medium akadama which will be the main soil ingredient.

4 Cut away the roots of the two largest plants on one side in preparation for placing them close together.

5 Place the two plants next to each other, with their roots pushed closely together.

6 Using 3mm (⅛in) wire, tie the first tree into the pot by twisting the ends of the wire tightly together with a pair of pliers.

7 Tie the second tree in place, close to the first, so that their bases are almost touching. ▷

8 After cutting the roots to fit, tie in the third tree, making sure that it is very closely positioned alongside the first two.

9 Wire all the trees firmly into the pot, so that they are all very secure because new roots will easily break if the trees are loose in the pot.

10 Here, all three of the trees have been securely wired into place.

11 Top up the soil using a scoop and then work the soil in and around the roots with a chopstick until the pot is completely filled.

12 The three trees are now finally planted and secured in the pot.

13 Prune out any unwanted shoots and branches, thus creating a pleasing shape.

14 After careful wiring and shaping, the triple trunk now looks relatively mature.

Right: *When complete, the group of trees should look like a full-size natural group of trees. Here, the triple-trunk planting has been improved by displaying it on a good-quality mahogany stand.*

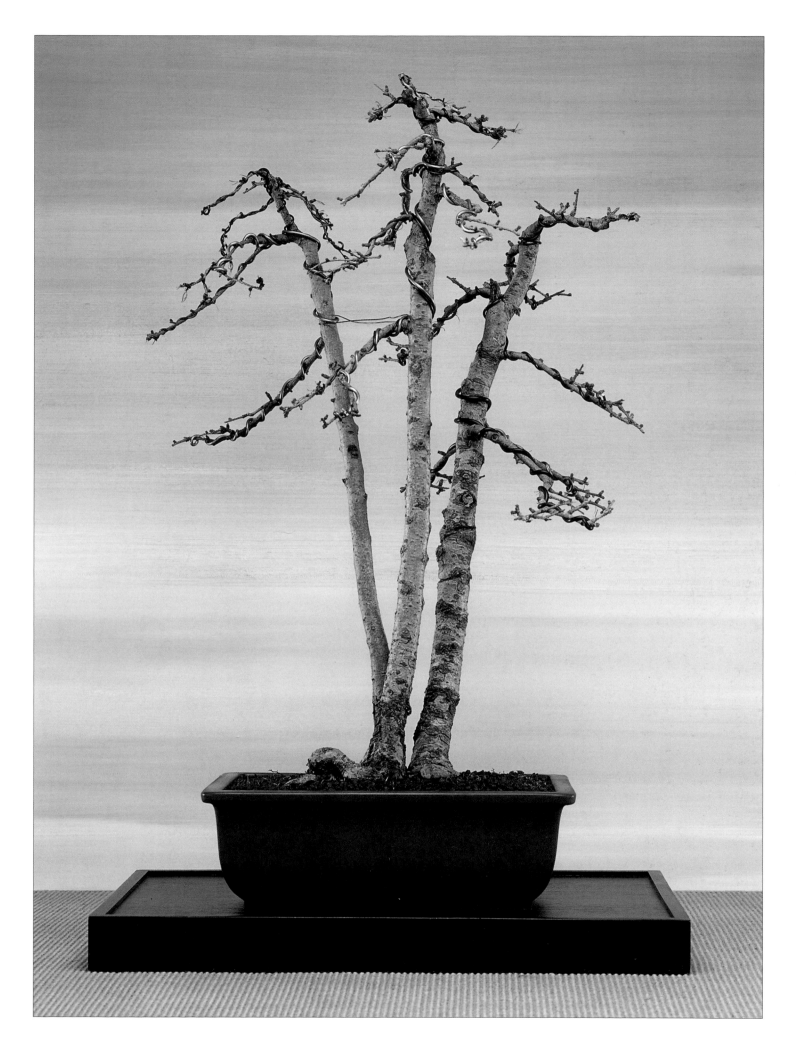

Group or Forest – *YOSE-UYE*

This style of bonsai planting is intended to create the appearance of a copse, spinney, small wood or even a large forest, only in miniature. A group or forest can be created using anything from five to fifty or more trees; in fact, you can use as many trees as can be satisfactorily handled. The only stipulation is that there should be an odd number of trees in order to lend a more balanced appearance to the final design. Your aim should be to create a group that gives the viewer the feeling of being within a wooded area, while being aware that it will be viewed from the outside. It may take several plantings to achieve this effect. Most types of plant are suitable, but, by keeping to the same species and variety for each group, you will achieve a more natural appearance.

Above: *A pot of beech plants – here* Fagus sylvatica *'Purpurea' – which are usually supplied for planting a hedge and are normally very inexpensive to purchase.*

Aim for a feeling of authenticity by obtaining a good sense of depth and perspective. Preferably, the group should not include any straight line of three trees or more, and no trunk should be hidden behind another when viewed from the front or side.

Make sure there is good mix of sizes to achieve a natural look. Also, choose one tree that is larger than the rest to act as a focal point. Note that branches may need to be removed from all the trees so they can sit closely together and not become confused with each other.

Starting with the largest tree, remove the lowest branches before positioning it in the prepared pot, just to the right or left of the centre and about halfway back. Place the second largest tree close to the first tree, removing branches as necessary. Then, position the rest of the trees, preferably one at a time, close to each other so that they form a natural-looking group or forest. Place the smaller trees on the outside of the group, but generally not at the front, so that the group appears to have been growing for many years.

Secure the trees into the container as you work, and fill in with soil by working it around the roots with a chopstick. Water thoroughly to settle the soil and trees into the container. Trim any remaining long shoots to give a balanced appearance, then place the completed group outdoors in a shady spot to acclimatize.

CREATING YOUR GROUP OR FOREST BONSAI

You will need
- Scissors
- Branch cutters
- Wire cutters
- Pliers
- Rake
- Pot
- Mesh
- Wire
- Soil
- Scoop
- Chopstick

1 One individual beech plant, showing the slim trunk, which is so suitable for group plantings, and with a good root system.

2 Remove any insignificant roots high on the trunk, thus creating a clean lower trunk.

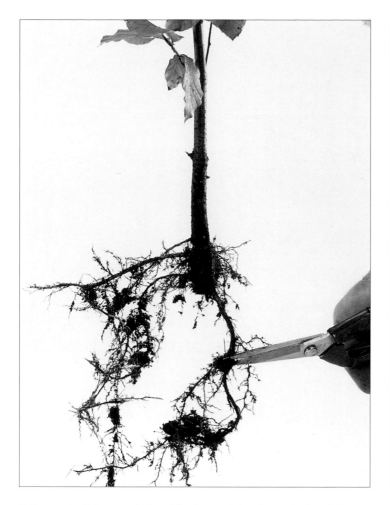

3 Now, cut off the remainder of the tap root, leaving a cluster of fibrous roots near the required trunk base.

4 Tidy up the remaining roots in order to leave a small, neat set of roots. The roots of all the plants to be used in the group should be treated in the same way.

5 Prepare a shallow pot and add some initial soil. The first two beech plants will be placed to the right of the centre and at about the half-way point from front to back.

6 Plunge the two plants into the soil and then work in some soil around them.

7 The plants may not be very stable at this stage, but when all the plants are in place, they will support each other.

▷

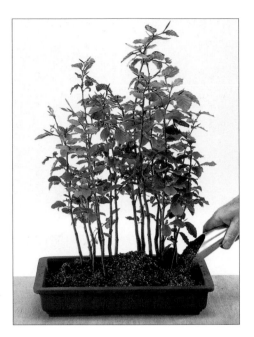

8 Add three more beech plants, making a total of five in all, and again work the roots down into the soil.

9 Using a scoop, add some extra soil around the roots of all five of the plants. It should be noted that the plants are inserted very close to each other. This needs to be done to make the final bonsai group look realistic.

10 When all fifteen plants have been introduced, more soil is added until the pot is full. The plants in this group are roughly arranged in two closely related sub-groups, with all trees set very close together.

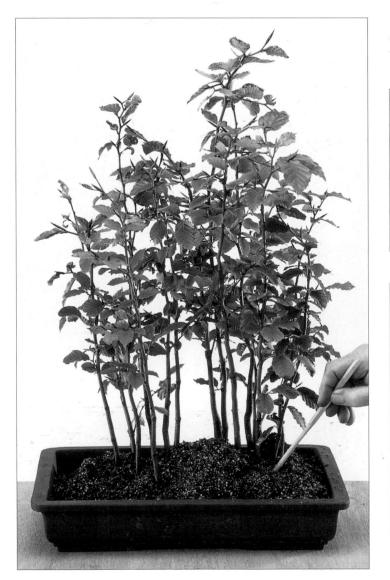

11 Use a chopstick to work the soil thoroughly around the roots of the plants, so that there is good contact with the soil throughout the root system.

12 The appearance of the top of the group can be improved by carefully selecting and removing any unsightly shoots that may be too long and look out of place.

13 The final grouping shows the close relationship of all the plants. This positioning is necessary if you are to achieve a natural-looking group or forest.

Right: *When complete, the group will begin to look like a small mature copse. The pot shown is temporary to encourage the trees' root development. Pots for bonsai groups must be shallow, and either oval or rectangular in shape.*

Windswept — *FUKINAGASHII*

On clifftops or mountains, trees grow in many different ways, but mostly in a windswept style caused by constant exposure to the prevailing winds coming from just one direction. Such trees will generally have a slanting trunk, with branches only on the leeward side of the trunk where the forces of nature are less harsh. Many trees in these situations have straight trunks with only the top part curved over away from the direction of the wind. Virtually any plant is suitable for creating a bonsai in the windswept style, although one with a leaning trunk would be easier if you are a beginner.

A straight trunk may be used, but it would have to tilt to give the impression of a wind-battered tree. The main interest of a tree like this is that the branch structure sweeps in one direction, which is the same direction as the one in which the trunk is leaning.

Suitable trees for the windswept style are pines, junipers, or tough deciduous trees such as hawthorn. These varieties are capable not only of surviving in a harsh natural habitat, but also of being manipulated, pruned and wired to form a windswept bonsai.

When selecting a suitable plant, check the root structure to find a plant which has strong roots on one side. This will then become the side that is opposite to the lean of the trunk because, in nature, the roots would develop a stronger structure on that side in order to support the leaning tree.

Remove the branches on what will appear to be the windward side of the trunk, along with any other insignificant branches. Position the remaining branches, fixing them in place with wire to obtain a mature

Above: This Juniperus chinensis *has been grown as a bonsai for several years and is now suitable for styling as a windswept-style bonsai.*

windswept feeling. Once the tree has been prepared, plant it in a suitable pot, tie it in place, top it up with soil and water in well.

Pots for this style of bonsai are generally round and shallow, but may have a rough, primitive finish, reflecting the fact that natural trees of this style would often exist in similarly rough surroundings.

CREATING YOUR WINDSWEPT BONSAI

You will need
- Branch cutters
- Scissors
- Wire cutters
- Pliers
- Rake
- Pot
- Mesh
- Wire
- Soil
- Scoop
- Chopstick

1 When viewed from a lower angle, it can be seen that the branches are all growing in one direction, indicating that a windswept design is possible.

Right: The bonsai is displayed on a suitable base and against a sympathetic background so that the final design can be fully appreciated. The tree will need several years of work before it is fully developed.

3 Following the process of wiring and positioning all of the branches, the windswept form is even more accentuated.

2 When the pot is tilted slightly to the rear and left using a suitable block, the potential of the windswept design for this particular specimen becomes even more apparent.

4 The tree has been repotted at a different angle to complete the windswept design.

Raft – *IKADABUKI*

The raft or straight-line style is based upon a natural phenomenon that occurs when a tree is blown over. Although the trunk of the tree lies flat on the ground, it may survive if some of the roots remain attached and viable. Many of the branches will have been broken off when the tree hit the ground, leaving that side of the trunk in contact with the soil. Eventually, roots will emerge from here, while the remaining branches begin to grow into a vertical position. After many years, the original broken roots will have rotted away, and what remains will look like several trees growing together.

Above: *This is a Chinese juniper (*Juniperus chinensis*) that has been previously grown as a bonsai and is ideal for styling as a raft-style bonsai, as can be seen from the fact that the branches are all on one side of the trunk.*

When looking for a suitable plant, ideally choose one that has a one-sided branch structure, which will mean less pruning to achieve the raft style. If this is not possible, purchase a tree that has a good set of branches, and remove all the branches on one side of the trunk.

Lay the tree down on the branchless side of the trunk, and use scissors to remove the roots that are now revealed at the base of the upper side of the trunk. Removing half the root system will not harm the tree, as half the branches have already been removed.

In fact, this equal pruning of branches and roots will ensure a balanced regrowth of the plant. If you need to remove more than half the root system for aesthetic purposes, then you should also remove a roughly equal number of branches to balance the plant and so ensure its survival.

Next, select the best remaining branches to be the new set of trunks, removing any that will not suit the shape. You will probably have to wire all the branches and place them in a more suitable, near-vertical, position

to create a group-like appearance. Finally, select the most suitable secondary branches (removing the rest), position them with wire and trim branch tips where necessary.

The most widely used pots for this style are long, narrow and oval. Thin slabs of slate or rock may also be used.

CREATING YOUR RAFT

You will need
- Rake
- Branch cutters
- Scissors
- Knife
- Wire cutters
- Pliers
- Wire
- Scoop
- Chopstick
- Wound sealer
- Pot
- Mesh
- Soil

1 The congested root system is apparent and needs to be raked, untangled and pruned so that a manageable amount of root remains.

2 Having raked away most of the soil and untangled the roots, cut back the roots until a compact pad of roots remains.

3 It is necessary to remove squares of bark on the lower side of the trunk. When this side of the trunk is beneath the surface of the soil, roots will grow around the edges of the removed squares of bark.

4 Cut into the bark using a sharp knife and then peel away the squares of bark in order to leave exposed areas of the heartwood.

5 Six pieces of bark have been removed. This should result in six areas of root growth on the underside of the trunk following planting in the soil.

6 Begin the shaping process by wiring the trunk and all of the main branches of the tree.

7 In this close-up, it can be seen that some of the wires run from one branch to another. This will ensure that the wire is properly anchored, so that the branches remain in the desired position.

▷

8 The initial wiring is complete and the relationship between the old trunk, which will form the new root system, and the old branches that will be the new trunks, is now becoming clear.

9 A long, shallow pot has been prepared with securing wires and a base layer of soil. The tree is then lowered into position.

10 Press the tree into the surface of the soil using gentle side-to-side movements. Bring the ends of the wires together in pairs.

11 Twist the ends of the wires together with a pair of pliers, pulling at the same time, so that you can be certain that the tree is securely fixed in the pot.

12 Make sure that the pairs of wire ends are twisted and pulled tight because this will enable the new roots to grow without disturbance.

13 Top up the pot with soil using a scoop and work the soil into and around the existing root system, as well as the old trunk that is now below the surface of the soil.

14 Water the completed raft arrangement thoroughly, using a watering can that has been fitted with a fine rose attachment. This will ensure that the soil is not disturbed.

15 This is the completed raft arrangement following the tidying of the surface of the soil and careful watering.

Above: *The smaller branches have now been wired and carefully manipulated into their final position. What was once a rather* *insignificant-looking plant has been transformed into a root-connected group that is commonly known as a raft.*

Root-in-Rock Planting – *ISHIZUKI*

Throughout the world, there are many places where trees can be seen growing on, over or in rock formations. It will have taken many years for the roots, often exposed over parts of the rock, to have grown into extremely interesting formations. It is these naturally occurring forms, when reproduced for the purposes of bonsai, that can create a very natural and inspirational design. Three variations of rock planting are commonly used in bonsai. These are "root-on-rock", "root-over-rock" and "root-in-rock". The name for each style aptly describes the placing of the roots relative to the piece of rock.

Achieving this style relies upon finding a suitable plant, as well as a matching piece of rock. The roots will be on the surface of the rock and covered with soil and moss; they will not necessarily carry on down to soil level. The roots grow in an artificially created or natural hole or crevice in the rock, which contains all the roots as well as the soil in which they grow.

Start with a piece of tufa (a porous sedimentary limestone that is easy to carve with a chisel or spatula), and make a hollow for the plant's roots.

Choose a small plant with a compact root-ball (roots) that will fit inside the hollow. Place a layer of soil in the cavity, then plant the tree in it, firming it in and topping up with extra soil until the plant is secure. Trim the plant and remove any unwanted branches to give the appearance of a naturally formed composition.

You may need to feed this type of bonsai more often than is normally the case because rain and regular watering will wash away the nutrients quite quickly.

Above: *This piece of tufa already has one hole in a suitable position for growing a cascade-style tree. You will need a couple of plants; here,* Juniperus procumbens *'Nana' has been used. The first plant has had its roots trimmed ready to fit the hole.*

Tufa retains water for some time, but does not waterlog the roots growing in the rock. Stand the tufa in a shallow basin of water so that the water is absorbed slowly. This will help with watering because of the water-retentive quality of tufa.

You will need
- Rock
- Soil
- Branch cutters
- Scissors
- Knife
- Scoop
- Chopstick
- Moss
- Basin

CREATING YOUR ROOT-IN-ROCK BONSAI

1 Using your fingers, carefully press the root-ball of the plant into the hole until it is securely in place. Fill in the cavity with soil.

2 Using a sharp pair of cutters, remove all the branches, except those that are cascading down over the side of the rock.

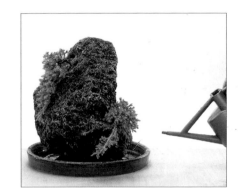

3 Here, it is clear which branches need to be pruned so that only downward-growing branches remain in place.

4 With the piece of rock standing in its finished position, offer up the second plant to ascertain where the second hole needs to be placed.

5 Tufa is very soft and is easily carved using a spatula or other similar instrument. Make sure that the hole is large enough to receive the roots of the second plant.

6 Gently press the second plant into position, filling in any spaces around the roots of both plants with soil. Place a layer of moss over the soil of both trees in order to complete the natural effect.

7 The completed planting can then be placed in a shallow basin which has been filled with water. As tufa is very porous, it will absorb enough water to suit the needs of the plants.

8 Allow the two plants to settle in for several weeks until the roots begin to grow into the porous tufa. At a later date, the two trees can be wired into shape so that they closely follow the contour of the rock.

Right: *The two trees, having been planted in the tufa, will require several years to reach maturity.*

Root-over-Rock Planting – *SEKIJOJU*

This style can be achieved by choosing a tree that has a long root system and washing away all the soil to expose the roots. If such a tree cannot be found, encourage the roots of your chosen plant to grow by placing it in a very long temporary container, such as a plastic tree guard, until the roots reach the bottom. Then, remove the tree from the tube and spread the roots over a piece of rock with an interesting shape until they fit closely to it. Tie the roots securely to the rock using wire. The preparation of a plant for root-over-rock planting can take several years, as the process of producing the long roots can be very slow, but, once you have achieved your first set of long roots, it is rewarding to know that it really can be done. This will encourage you to try something bigger and better.

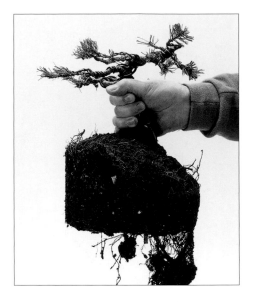

Above: *This mountain pine,* Pinus mugo *'Pumilio', underwent extensive wiring and shaping several weeks prior to this exercise and has been allowed enough time to settle in before the next stage of the process.*

Plant the chosen tree – here a *Pinus mugo* 'Pumilio' – in a deep container, covering the whole root-ball (roots), including the rock, with some soil. Over the next few years, the roots will expand and develop a close fit with the rock, appearing to cascade over it. This means that when the rock is eventually exposed, a very interesting root structure should have developed that follows its contours.

This style is probably one of the most difficult of all the bonsai designs to tackle and ultimately perfect because, while the roots are maturing under the surface of the soil, it is not possible to know what, if anything, is actually happening.

However, you should rest assured that, given sufficient time, the roots of the tree will eventually thicken and become attached, as well as cross over with other roots. The roots will also become naturally grafted to each other while they are submerged beneath the soil. Time is perhaps one of the most important considerations for the successful development of this style.

Patience will also be necessary because it is a serious mistake to uncover the roots too soon. It is crucial that they stay covered with soil if they are to enlarge correctly.

The container for this style should be rugged in appearance to suit the ruggedness of the rock.

You will need
- Hook
- Rock
- Wire cutters
- Wire
- Branch cutters
- Scissors
- Pliers
- Rake
- Scoop
- Chopstick
- Pot
- Mesh
- Soil
- Sphagnum moss

CREATING YOUR ROCK-OVER-ROOT PLANTING BONSAI

1 Following the removal of the lower half of the root-ball (roots), rake out the rest of the roots using a suitable single hook.

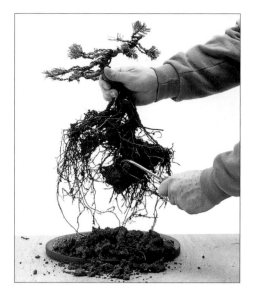

2 Rake away the rest of the soil until the roots are free of soil.

3 Wash the roots thoroughly using a low-pressure water jet from a garden hose.

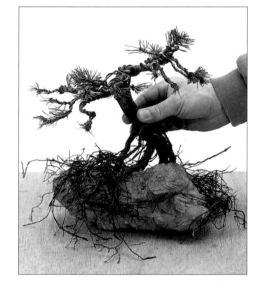

4 You need to wash the roots very thoroughly, so that they can be placed easily and cleanly over the rock.

5 Carefully spread out the roots by hand and then place them over the rock.

6 Press the roots into place so that they straddle as many sides of the rock as possible.

7 Using a length of 3mm (⅛in) wire, tie the tree firmly to the rock and secure by twisting the two ends of the wire together.

▷

8 Wind a longer length of 3mm (⅛in) wire several times around the roots, securing them all in close proximity with the rock, and again twist the ends together.

9 Choose a pot that is large enough to accept the whole rock-and-root system, and place a layer of soil in the bottom.

10 Press the rock, complete with the roots, into the soil, making sure that the top of the rock does not come above the level of the pot rim, and fill in with soil.

11 Add a layer of sphagnum moss to the surface of the soil in order to keep the surface roots moist and soft.

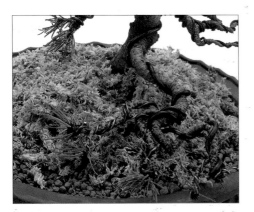

12 Covering the surface of the soil completely with moss is absolutely essential.

13 Following the planting of the whole rock into the pot, the project is now complete, but it will take several years for the roots to grow in close contact with the rock. Eventually, the rock and the roots around it will be exposed.

Right: *The completed tree is finally placed in a temporary pot with the roots and rock below the surface of the soil.*

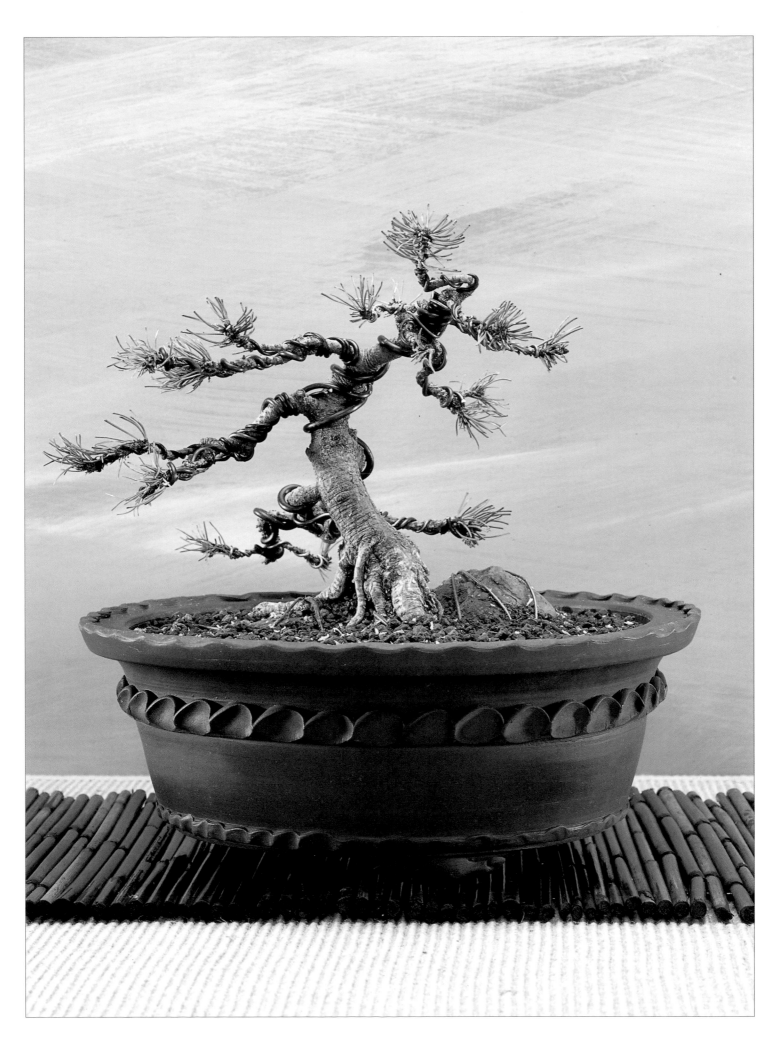

Literati – *BUNJIN*

This is an unusual style which does not conform to the general rules of bonsai styling. It often appears in nature when a number of trees have grown together over many years, and then some have died or been removed, leaving just a few individual trees. These trees will have grown tall in the stiff competition for available light, and the resulting foliage will be on or near the top of the trees. Examples of this style growing in the wild are often pines. This style of tree can also be seen growing with tall, slim, freestyle-type trunks, with just a few branches positioned quite high up on the tree. The literati style is a very useful one because it can be used to make a bonsai from almost any plant that is tall and gangly, and which does not fit into any other bonsai category.

Above: *This Scots pine (*Pinus sylvestris*) was collected from the wild and grown in a temporary timber training box. It is partially wired and styled, and shown here from its best angle before final styling.*

Trees in the literati style normally have a tall, slim, free-style trunk, often with very little taper, culminating in a small number of branches in the apex of the tree. The trunk is very important: it is almost never straight and should be full of character, with slight twists and turns, although nothing too accentuated.

When you are choosing a tree that is suitable for turning into a literati bonsai, you will need to find one that may have been neglected, damaged, or both, making it unsuitable for any other style. It need not have a particularly good surface root system, as in nature this type of tree tends to grow that way; in fact, they appear to rise straight from the soil with very little visible support. If you intend to start from scratch, making the branches droop severely means that the effect of considerable age can be easily achieved.

Most conifers, but particularly pines (*Pinus*), will make good literati. In fact, it is species or varieties of this genus that seem to adopt the literati shape when growing naturally in the wild.

As this style is tall and slender, suitable pots would be circular, relatively shallow and not too large, as anything too big could overpower the elegant but rugged character of the trees. A rather rough, primitive pot would be suitable for this style, as it would enhance its rugged nature.

You will need
- Branch cutters
- Scissors
- Wire cutters
- Pliers
- Rake
- Pot
- Mesh
- Wire
- Soil
- Scoop
- Chopstick

CREATING YOUR LITERATI BONSAI

1 Close-up of the triple-wiring technique used during the application of the wire.

2 The appearance of the triple-wiring technique after the application of the wire.

3 View of the right-hand side of the partially wired and styled tree.

4 The rear of the partially wired and styled pine showing the extent of branch repositioning.

5 Following the wiring of all the branches, this is now the preferred front of the tree.

6 The left-hand side of the tree after wiring and shaping.

7 Rear view of the tree after final wiring and shaping.

8 Right-hand side of the tree after the final wiring and shaping process. The tree is now beginning to take on the shape of an old mature specimen.

Right: *The finished styled bonsai has been repotted into a drum pot, which is ideally suited to the literati style.*

Driftwood – *SHARIMIKI*

The driftwood style is considered a more advanced technique. It reflects the natural look of old junipers and pines, which have areas of trunk that are totally free of bark. In the wild, this is caused by natural die-back or by lightning. Whatever the cause, the result can be dramatic and exciting. This style can be formed by taking a plant with a thick trunk and stripping part of the bark away to create the driftwood. It can also be formed by using a piece of suitable driftwood and attaching a younger plant to it. This is often called a "wraparound" as the living material is simply wrapped around a piece of dead wood.

Driftwood techniques can be used in several other styles of bonsai, including the literati, informal upright, cascade and windswept styles. If you are going to create a driftwood-style bonsai from a single plant, then you will need one that has a thick trunk so that you can strip away the bark from the main trunk to form the basis of the driftwood.

A much simpler method is to use a piece of collected driftwood or perhaps even the dead trunk of an old bonsai.

If you use the latter, then treat it with a wood preservative which will soak completely into the dead wood. This may need to be repeated several times over a period of months to make sure that the wood is properly protected against the normal decaying process that wood undergoes, particularly when wet. The piece of treated wood will then need to be left to dry thoroughly, so that all traces of any unsafe liquids in the preservative have evaporated away.

Above: *A* Cedrus deodara *nursery plant and a piece of driftwood, both of which are suitable for creating a driftwood-style bonsai.*

You will need various tools for attaching the plant to the driftwood, including stainless-steel screws, raffia and wire, as well as a power drill. When using power tools, follow the manufacturer's safety guidelines.

Suitable pots for this style vary, but as the form is rugged and primitive, the pot should reflect these qualities.

CREATING YOUR DRIFTWOOD BONSAI

You will need
- Branch cutters
- Knife
- Rake
- Sprayer
- Screwdriver
- Screws
- Raffia
- Wire cutters
- Wire
- Scissors
- Pot
- Mesh
- Soil
- Scoop
- Chopstick

1 Remove the shoots and branches completely on one side of the plant and, using a sharp knife, cut away approximately half of the trunk on the side from which the branches have been removed.

2 Rake out the root-ball (roots) in order to remove excess soil, and trim the roots into a compact system. Spray the roots regularly to prevent them drying out because this style takes a long time to produce. Using a power tool or hand screwdriver, attach the lower trunk to the lower part of the driftwood. Stainless-steel screws are preferable, but brass would be a good second choice.

3 Continue to attach the trunk with screws, making sure that the cut side of the trunk sits adjacent to the driftwood.

4 The trunk can be curved around to the front of the driftwood so that it follows any curving features of the driftwood, and then secured with raffia.

5 When the trunk becomes too narrow to accept a screw, continue to attach it to the driftwood by tying it tightly with raffia.

6 While you are attaching the plant to the driftwood, keep spraying the roots regularly and cover them with a plastic bag to retain moisture. This will assist the tree during the lengthy attachment process.

▷

7 The tree is planted in a suitable pot and secured firmly with wire as described in the repotting section. The most exposed and best-looking part of the driftwood normally forms the front of the bonsai.

8 Some of the branches are removed, with the remaining branches being wired and carefully manipulated into place to create a tree-like shape.

9 With the wiring and shaping now complete, any downward-growing foliage is removed in order to leave the tree with a tidy and compact shape.

11 Close-up of the top of the tree, showing the raffia attachment and branch wiring in detail.

12 The interesting structure of the lower part of the driftwood which will eventually be the main lower trunk of the finished bonsai.

10 This is the back of the driftwood on the upper part of the tree, showing the position of the trunk and branch in relation to it.

Right: *The finished styling shows the basic shape of the tree. This will be enhanced over the following years as the foliage areas bulk out and the real bonsai emerges.*

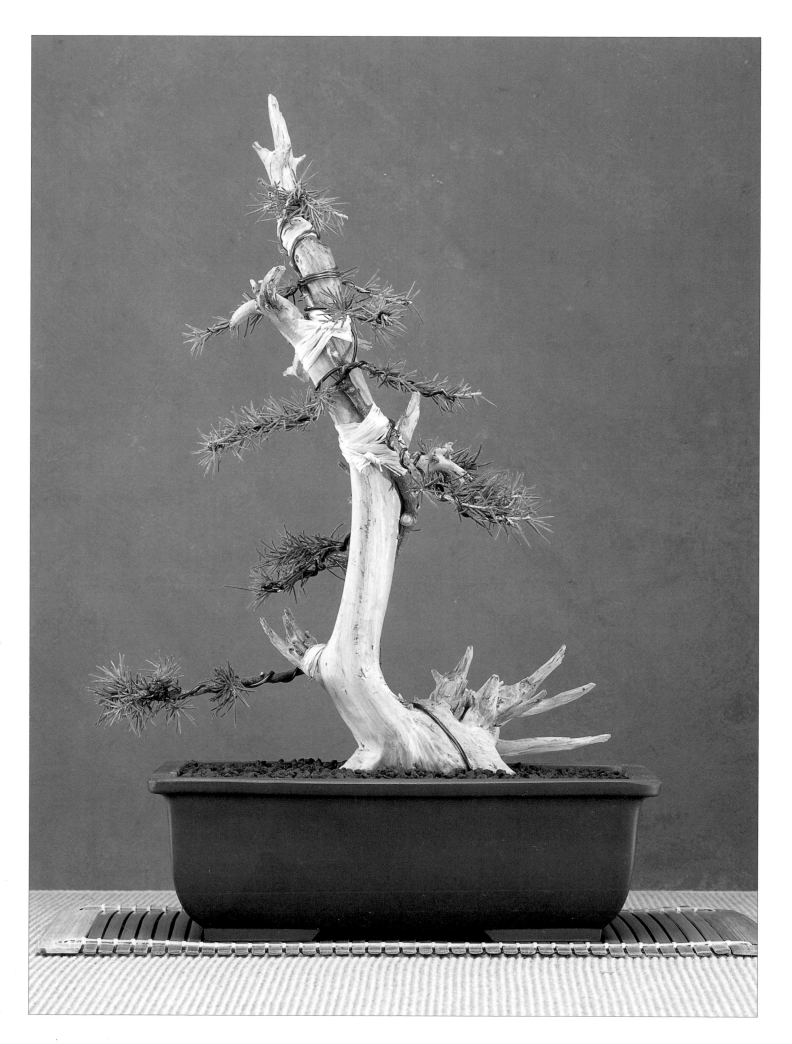

Twisted Trunk — *NEJKAN*

This style clearly has a very strong Chinese connection because it is followed by many Chinese bonsai artists. Indeed, ancient Chinese artefacts often contain paintings of trees such as this. Many different types of plants can be trained in this style of bonsai, but it is obviously advisable to choose a variety that has a very flexible trunk so that its shape can easily be altered with a suitable application of wire. Once the wire has been added, it is then possible to manipulate the trunk line into virtually any shape you wish, as long as the trunk is flexible enough. The structure of the branches is then styled so that they blend well with the line of the trunk.

Above: *A mountain pine (Pinus mugo) which has been grown in a shallow container for several years to obtain a shallow root system suitable for bonsai training.*

The twisted trunk is not a very popular style for bonsai because it does not have a particularly natural appearance. The trunk is actually spiral-shaped, and this can be achieved by using thick wire to manipulate it into place. You will need a tree with a fairly thick trunk that is flexible enough to be curved into the required shape. Use a rake to scrape away the surface soil so that you can check the healthiness of the root system and establish which is the best side to form the front. Select branches that will make a natural-looking tree.

Using branch or knob cutters, remove any unwanted branches so that the full trunk line is exposed. The complete tree is then wired with wires of an appropriate thickness, so that the structure can be formed by gently bending the branches. Always make sure that a single piece of wire is used to travel from the branch around the trunk and along another so that two branches can be anchored by each other. It is important to wire all branches, however large or small, so that every single part of the tree can be worked into a suitable position. This will ultimately result in a design that is pleasing to the eye.

When the final shape of the bonsai has been achieved, you will need to trim back all the shoot tips lightly in order to encourage the generation of more new buds within the inner parts of the tree.

CREATING YOUR TWISTED TRUNK BONSAI

You will need
- Branch cutters
- Scissors
- Wire
- Wire cutters
- Rake
- Pot
- Mesh
- Soil
- Scoop

1 Tilt the tree by resting the rear of the root-ball on the back edge of the seed tray. This will give a better appearance to the line of the trunk.

2 Use branch cutters to remove the branch that is obscuring the front trunk-line of the tree.

4 Using branch cutters, prune out any long, uninteresting branches.

5 Wire the remaining branches and carefully bend them into place.

3 Cut out all the minor inner branches with a pair of scissors, so that the full extent of the twisted-trunk line is shown at its best.

6 Bend the rest of the branches into place, and trim away excessively long shoots to refine the outline.

Right: *Following the completion of the styling, the bonsai is placed in a pot that reflects the curvaceous nature of the tree.*

Exposed Root – *NEAGARI*

The roots of many trees in the wild are uncovered by years of exposure to natural elements such as rain and wind. Indeed, some elderly trees have a large number of roots exposed, so that the tree looks as if it is standing on stilts. In the world of bonsai, these natural features can be artificially created by growing roots specially for the purpose, but it is easier for novices in the art and culture of bonsai to acquire a plant that already has thickened roots. When visiting plant centres or bonsai nurseries, you will need to examine the root systems of your potential purchase, but be careful not to disturb them too much, unless you are confident that you will buy the tree, because the staff may not be pleased. As with all bonsai, the appearance of this style can be improved by adding some moss to the surface of the soil.

In the exposed-root style, you are trying to copy a natural feature, as you are with all bonsai, whatever the style. Indeed, the first task you must carry out to turn a garden-centre plant into a bonsai is to rake the surface soil away from the roots to expose some of them. This gives the lower part of the tree a mature and established look. You should find a tree that has long, mature roots by probing into the soil before you buy. Virtually any species of tree may be used and a suitable pot would be simple and rugged.

The exposed part of the root system now technically becomes part of the bonsai trunk and must be treated in the same way as normal. The exposed roots will need to be kept clean and free of the moss that will slowly cover the lower part of the trunk if it is not kept in check. A stiff brush, such as an old toothbrush, is ideal for this purpose, but bonsai suppliers will also have a range of suitable brushes that will allow you to access narrow gaps between some of the exposed roots.

Above: *This trident maple (*Acer buergerianum*) has been purchased from a bonsai nursery. It is highly suited to the exposed-root style.*

Some people are tempted to fill the gap in the exposed-root system with a rock of some kind, but this will only turn your exposed-root bonsai into a root-over-rock style and would defeat the original purpose. It would be acceptable to add a rock alongside the tree, but do not fill in any gaps between the roots.

CREATING YOUR EXPOSED ROOT BONSAI

You will need
- Rake
- Brush
- Root shears
- Scissors
- Pot
- Mesh
- Wire
- Soil
- Scoop
- Chopstick

1 Remove the tree from the pot, taking care not to damage the branches because they can be quite brittle in a trident maple.

2 Rake the soil away to expose the thickened roots that will become the exposed part of the bonsai root system.

3 Brush the main roots clean, using a stiff brush, until the mature part of the root-ball (roots) is completely exposed.

4 Trim the fibrous root-ball with root shears so that the bottom is neat and flat. This will help you to fit the tree into a suitably sized bonsai pot.

5 Settle the tree into a prepared pot with the best roots to the front.

6 Fill the pot with soil using a scoop, and work it around the roots with a chopstick.

Above: *When the roots are securely placed in the pot, the appearance of the soil surface can be improved with the application of some moss to make the finished tree look more natural.*

Clump – *KABUBUKI OR KABUDACHI*

There are several ways that this design can be created, but the most common involves gathering several young trees together and tying them tightly at the base for several years so that they naturally graft together. You must make sure that the trees do not become strangulated. If it looks as though this is likely to happen, then the tie should be released and another applied. This style can be seen quite often in the wild, usually in woodland areas where many seeds have germinated, grown in close proximity, and then grafted together over a number of years. It is a very simple bonsai style to create because it needs little in the way of materials, tools and spare time. Simple young plants will be ideal to use, as they will grow rapidly to produce the desired result.

Above: *Five common beech (*Fagus sylvatica*) hedging plants, which are suitable for creating a clump-style bonsai.*

There are very many plant varieties that are suitable for this fairly simple style. Deciduous trees are recommended in particular because they graft together more easily than coniferous plants. For beginners to bonsai, it would be much better to start with young plants that can be easily obtained from your local plant centre. Small self-seeded plants would also make ideal plant material, but they may be smaller than those plants that are commercially available and your bonsai would take longer to mature.

If you are a little more ambitious, the process described can be carried out on very much larger plants, which will provide a more challenging, and possibly more interesting, final design. You will need a more substantial tying mechanism, such as wire, to hold all the plants together and a larger pot to accommodate the root system.

As with any bonsai styling and arrangement process, you will need to be very patient because the growth rate of plants can vary considerably. Young plants tend to graft together quickly,

while older plants will inevitably be very much slower. Always take your time when constructing any bonsai arrangement and never allow the roots to dry out completely. Simply make sure that you have a water spray to hand, so that regular applications of water can be made to the roots. This will enhance the survival rate of the bonsai following completion.

CREATING YOUR CLUMP BONSAI

You will need
- Rake
- Scissors
- Raffia
- Pot
- Mesh
- Wire
- Wire cutters
- Soil
- Scoop
- Chopstick

1 Remove any roots that appear high up on the trunk, leaving radial roots for development.

2 Remove the thick tap roots completely, so that only fine fibrous roots remain. This will encourage more fibrous roots to develop.

3 Shorten the remaining fibrous roots, leaving a reasonable amount to ensure the survival of the plant.

4 All five plants have been root-pruned and are now ready for assembly into the initial clump design.

5 Using a length of raffia, tie the five tightly together immediately above the root system of each plant.

▷

6 Prepare a shallow, oval pot and then add some soil before carefully placing the clump of trees in the soil.

7 The roots should be worked well into the soil, so that the raffia is approximately level with the rim of the pot.

9 The initial styling of the clump-style bonsai is now complete. The clump will now need to grow and become more refined over several seasons before achieving its full potential as a bonsai.

8 Top up with dry soil using a scoop and work the soil into the root system using a chopstick. Water the arrangement well, allow it to drain and then keep in a shaded place for several weeks.

Right: *The finished clump has had the raffia disguised with soil and the completed planting is displayed on a dark wood stand against a suitable background. The five plants will mature so that they all eventually graft together at the base. At this point, the trunk base can be exposed.*

Broom – *HOKIDACHI*

This style looks similar to the traditional broom used for sweeping, which is made from a bunch of twigs tied to a wooden handle. As full-size trees, this style can be seen in parks and gardens all over the world. It was initially derived from the natural shape of several varieties of *Zelkova*. It is, therefore, best suited to these trees, but other species can also be successfully grown in this style. Deciduous trees in particular lend themselves to training into broom-style bonsai because they quickly produce a good array of branches that will form a tight, twiggy, upper structure to the tree. Frequent pinching of the leading shoots on all the branches throughout the growing season will lead to excellent branch ramification with very little physical effort.

Above: *An old elm tree* (Ulmus) *that has been prepared with air layering in readiness for developing into a new bonsai.*

The form is based around a straight section of trunk with the branches coming from the top. There may be a continuation of the initial part of the trunk, but it will taper fairly abruptly and have smaller branches emerging along its length.

As each branch is developed, it should take on a finely branched, twiggy form. Frequent pinching out of the shoot tips is one of the most important aspects of the year-by-year improvement of this style, so do not neglect this part of the process.

If the weekly shoot pinching through the growing season from mid-spring to late summer is missed, and the branches become too long, they can be reduced by pruning fairly hard and starting again. If this pinching is carried out regularly, then the emerging leaves will naturally be slightly smaller than the previous batch that have been removed by the pruning process. This means that as time goes by, a spectacular bonsai will develop, as long as the correct pruning regime has been followed.

Never forget that a bonsai will continue growing if it is not controlled. This is especially true of the broom as it depends on concentrated pruning every spring and summer to maintain a compact structure. As the bonsai matures, study it in the winter when it is free of foliage. This is the best time to remove branches that are becoming too dense or are causing confusion.

CREATING YOUR BROOM BONSAI

You will need
- Saw
- Wound sealer
- Branch cutters
- Scissors
- Rake
- Pot
- Mesh
- Wire
- Wire cutters
- Soil
- Scoop

1 Close-up of the root system produced during the air-layering technique. This is one year on from the initial preparation.

2 Using a saw, remove the air-layered section to leave a stump that will eventually produce many new shoots.

3 Cut the top of the stump into a "V" shape to encourage shoots to appear from slightly different positions around the trunk circumference.

4 Close-up of the "V"-cut, which will need to be sealed with a suitable wound sealing paste to assist the plant in the production of shoots. The plant will take some time to produce a suitable number of shoots.

5 On another elm that has already produced a suitable number of shoots, it can be seen how the initial development takes place.

6 The top of the stump needs to be tidied up using branch or knob cutters, and trimmed back to the uppermost shoots.

7 The lower shoots are removed using a pair of scissors until a group of shoots remains at the top of the trunk. The plant is then potted up in a temporary pot so that it can grow on and develop into a proper broom-style bonsai.

Above: *The remaining shoots are all growing at approximately the same level, albeit radiating out around the trunk. These will mature into a dense branch structure that will enhance the tree's appearance.*

INDOOR BONSAI

Most people, when starting out in the bonsai world, often keep their first bonsai indoors because it is a commonly held view that all bonsai are indoor plants. This misunderstanding normally leads to disaster and an instant withdrawal from the bonsai scene. Most bonsai are actually outdoor plants if they are kept in the correct conditions. However, if kept in areas outside their normal habitat, they will need special environmental conditions to ensure their survival. Tropical and subtropical plants will be classified as indoor bonsai when grown in colder areas of the world and temperate climate plants will need special environmental conditions if they are grown in hotter areas. In temperate climates, tropical and subtropical plants will always be called indoor bonsai, but it is not so easy to provide them with the warmer and more humid conditions they require. They will need good light, but not direct sunlight through a window, and a warm, slightly humid atmosphere.

Left: *A weeping fig (*Ficus benjamina *'Wiandii') in the early stages of training, showing the initial wiring process that will help in the formation of the final branch structure.*

Aralia elegantissima

These plants, commonly known as finger aralia, can have one or more trunks and make a very attractive landscape. *Aralia* is a member of the ivy family which consists of trees, shrubs and palm-like plants, some of which have spines. They often have woody stems, even the smaller varieties such as the one described here. This variety is ideally suited to a group situation, as it tends to be upright with a relatively slim trunk. When grouped fairly closely together, a very pleasant indoor forest can be achieved. These plants can be sourced quite easily from plant centres or nurseries and have a compact root structure suited to shallow containers.

When growing bonsai plants in a group, always make sure that the tallest plant is somewhere in the central third of the arrangement and that the rest of the plants get progressively smaller towards the sides and rear.

Trim away all lower side shoots so that the trunks or main stems can be clearly seen. As with all group plantings or forests, the plants should always be placed very close together in order to give a mature feeling to the arrangement. The plants can be split into two groups so that an impression is given of a footpath running through the forest.

Small stones or rocks can be included in the composition to give a more rugged feel to the group and moss or very small plants can be planted under the main trees to enhance the natural look of the forest.

Containers should be shallow and can be rectangular or oval. The pot should not be too bright in colour and should complement the foliage colour of the trees. As with all bonsai

Above: *Suitable* Aralia *plants can be bought from many plant centres and will be sold simply as houseplants; these can be quickly turned into an indoor-bonsai planting.*

containers, it should never clash with the trees in any way, but just be there for growing support and minimal decorative appearance. Pots normally have a subtle glaze or a matt (flat) finish and should, of course, have good-sized drainage holes.

As with all indoor bonsai, it is a good idea to mist regularly to maintain the health and vigour of the trees.

STYLING YOUR *ARALIA ELEGANTISSIMA*

You will need
- Scissors
- Pot
- Mesh
- Wire
- Wire cutters
- Soil
- Scoop
- Chopstick
- Rake
- Rocks

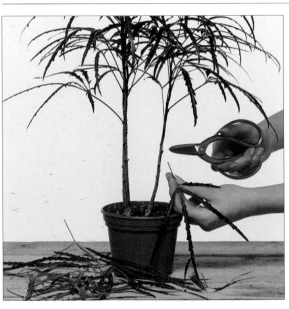

1 Cut off the lower and inner leaves of the plants using a pair of scissors, so that the trunks can be clearly seen. This will immediately open up the stems so that they look like trunks and create a more tree-like effect. It is surprising how different a simple plant can look when the main stem, or trunk, is cleared of foliage. This applies to almost any plant that has a woody stem, and is one of the first features you should look for when choosing a plant for a bonsai.

2 Place in the prepared pot, arranging the seven trunks so that they are slightly spread out at the top.

3 Add extra soil and work well in with a chopstick until the plants are firmly arranged in the pot. Press the soil well into the roots, but do not compact it too tightly because the roots will not be able to breathe.

4 Carefully position several pieces of rock or tufa to give the effect of a miniature landscape. Make sure the pieces of rock are firmly embedded in the soil so they look as if they have always been there. This will greatly enhance the overall appearance of the finished bonsai.

Right: *Once the styling is complete and a stone and some soil decoration have been put in place, the group makes a very attractive indoor bonsai that will give great pleasure as long as the soil is kept just moist at all times. Do not forget to mist spray the foliage regularly as this will help the tree to cope with the drier indoor atmosphere.*

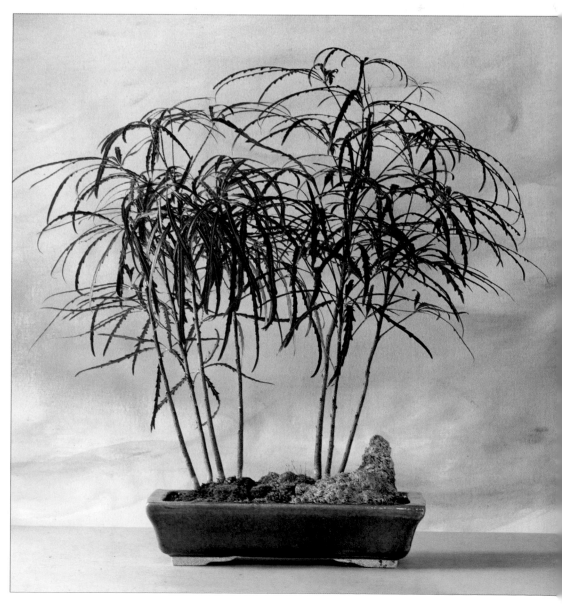

Crassula arborescens

Commonly known as the money tree or jade plant, this is often underestimated as bonsai material. Many species of crassula are available and *C. arborescens* is one of the best. There are many varieties available that have smaller leaves which may be even more suitable as bonsai. Most of them produce flowers at some time in the year and therefore can make very interesting indoor bonsai. Being succulents, they are prone to frosts that will almost certainly kill the plant in a very short time. Some are semi-hardy and may be suitable for cold conservatories (sun rooms) and greenhouses. Most, however, are quite happy outdoors providing they are slowly acclimatized. Crassula can be defoliated and pruned very hard if required and need very little water, so are ideal if they need to be left untended for several weeks.

Crassula arborescens has thick leaves and is strictly a succulent. The leaves and stems hold a large quantity of water, which allows the plant to go for several weeks without showing any signs of wilting. This characteristic makes the plant easy to look after as it needs watering less often than most plants. Even if it dries out, wilts and looks dehydrated, it will almost always recover once watering is resumed.

Propagation is also easy; just break off a leaf, leave until the end is dry (for about four days), and lay it on the surface of some dry soil. In about one month the leaf will have sprouted new roots. Do not water until you can see signs of new growth. Feed as with other houseplants, but only with a weak mixture of fertilizer.

When you are controlling the growth of your bonsai *Crassula*, you should wait until two or three pairs of leaves have been produced and then trim back to just one pair. Each time you do this, the growth pattern will double up. That is to say, each pruned shoot will produce two new shoots.

Above: *This is a typical garden centre or supermarket plant which can be trained into an attractive indoor bonsai.*

Never allow the plant to be exposed to frost, because its high water content will freeze and, on thawing, the tree will just collapse.

Overall, this is a very easy plant for bonsai because it has a compact root system that requires little water. The leaves will become overlarge if too much water is given, so keep watering to a minimum.

You will need
- Branch cutters
- Scissors
- Rake
- Pot
- Mesh
- Wire cutters
- Soil
- Scoop
- Chopstick

STYLING YOUR *CRASSULA ARBORESCENS*

1 Cut off the left-hand trunk using branch cutters, so that the main trunk in the centre is dominant.

2 Clean up the stump, using branch or knob cutters to form a natural-looking trunk base free from excess plant growth.

3 Pull off the lower leaves to expose the line of the tree's main trunk.

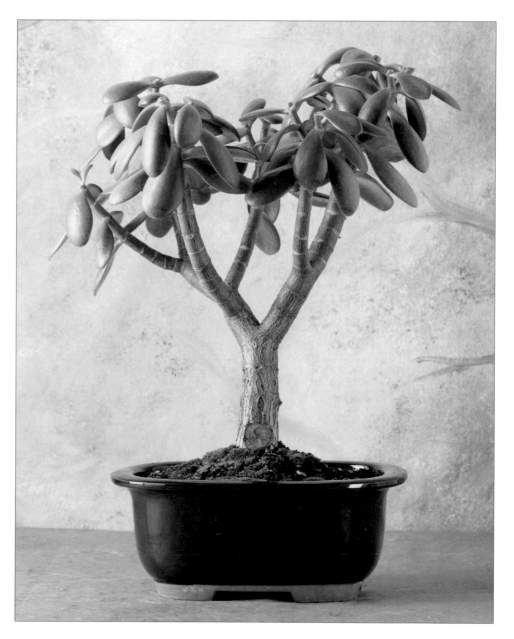

4 Having removed the leaves, it is clear that the other low branch should also be removed. This allows you to see the main trunk at its best.

5 Using scissors, reduce the length of the leading shoots.

6 Place in a suitable pot and top up with soil, working it in and around the roots with a chopstick until the soil fills every space.

Above: *Once the styled plant is complete, some moss can be added to the surface of the soil to give a more natural look which will enhance the line of the trunk. New shoots will soon begin to appear from the pruned shoot ends.*

Ficus benjamina 'Wiandii'

This *Ficus* has a compact growth habit and well-proportioned leaves. Plants may have one or more trunks and generally have an interesting root system. Regular misting of the foliage with water is beneficial and the soil should be kept just moist at all times. Feed lightly, but regularly, during the main growing season from spring to autumn. As the shoots grow, prune them back to one or two leaves. This plant will enjoy warm, humid conditions, so it would be ideal for keeping in a conservatory (sun room) or similar surroundings. It is fairly tolerant of slightly dry conditions when allied to higher humidity, as the humidity will help the survival of the relatively thick leaves. A negative aspect of this *Ficus* is that the branches can be brittle and so should be handled with care.

Above: Ficus benjamina *'Wiandii' can be bought from the indoor plant section of most plant centres or superstores. This is good material for training into an indoor bonsai because it is a tropical or semitropical plant.*

A serious point to note about *Ficus* is that, when pruned, the wounds will produce a sticky white latex solution that is toxic and should be kept away from the eyes and not ingested. This latex solution also appears when the plant is root pruned, so you should be cautious whenever pruning any part of this fig. Always wash your hands thoroughly after you have been working on these plants.

Many varieties and cultivars are now available, so the choice of a plant for bonsai culture is very wide-ranging. There are extremely drooping varieties, as well as more formal upright forms, some with very small rather thin leaves and some with very large, thick leaves. Variegated varieties are also very popular as houseplants, and these, too, will make very interesting and different additions to a bonsai collection.

Ficus can be purchased as single-trunk plants or multiple-trunk specimens in a wide range of sizes, so there should be something available to suit every bonsai grower's taste.

Figs can be shaped by pruning or wiring, but take care that you do not break the branches when you are manipulating them after wiring because they can be very brittle. As figs usually have smooth bark, they can be easily damaged if the wire is left on for too long, so check them regularly.

STYLING YOUR *FICUS BENJAMINA* 'WIANDII'

You will need
- Branch cutters
- Wound sealer
- Wire
- Wire cutters
- Scissors
- Rake
- Pot
- Mesh
- Soil
- Scoop
- Chopstick

1 Leaves growing directly from the trunk and branches must be removed to create a clean-looking plant. White latex fluid oozes from cut areas of the *Ficus* family and contact with the mouth or eyes should be avoided at all times.

2 A small amount of wiring has been carried out and excess shoots cut out in order to create a tree-like shape.

3 Use a sharp, clean pair of cutters to remove the excess shoots.

4 This is the final shape of the bonsai, before it is placed in a bonsai pot.

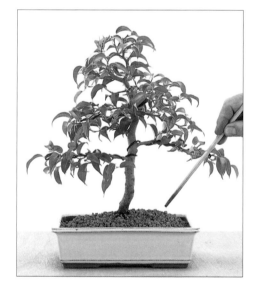

5 The tree has been repotted and the dry soil is being worked into the root system using a chopstick. After repotting, water the soil and allow any excess water to drain away.

Right: *The tree blends well with the cream glazed pot and has been displayed on a dark stand that shows the pot and tree to advantage.*

Myrtus communis

This variety is commonly known as dwarf myrtle, and only young plants are usually available, but it is relatively easy to train as bonsai. If you can buy some small plants, a miniature landscape can be constructed using a combination of plants, soil and rocks. Try to thin out the top growth to achieve a branched structure. It will be tempting to "clip" the foliage, but that would be topiary rather than bonsai. You will also need to be persistent with the thinning-out process because a dense mass of foliage can quickly regrow. Myrtle is relatively small-leaved in most of its forms and is therefore highly suited to this type of miniature landscape. The leaves will become substantially smaller with pruning and over time, and the plants will make attractive small bonsai that are suitable for grouping together.

This species requires regular misting to maintain the health of the foliage, particularly in the summer. As with most indoor bonsai, this variety can be placed outside in a shady spot in warmer weather. Water when the soil starts to dry out, but never allow the roots to stand in water as they will quickly rot. Good light is important, but do not place your tree in direct sunlight as this will scorch the leaves.

Because myrtles develop into compact bonsai easily, they can be planted in a variety of arrangements using different rock formations. They grow well in rocks as they have compact root systems and will fit into even the smallest of cavities. They would, however, be more suited to low-lying rockscapes as they generally grow into compact bush-like structures.

Try to be bold and use your imagination when planting any size or arrangement of landscape, as it is individual ideas that produce the great diversity of shapes and forms which make growing bonsai such an inspiring art form.

Above: *These are typical of commercially available* Myrtus communis *plants. They are small, compact and very suitable for constructing a small landscape planting.*

Pots or containers should be shallow and possibly slab-like in shape. If the pot is too deep, it will dominate the composition, so ensure that the pot is complementary to the bonsai and not overpowering. You will also need to add some ground-cover plants to give a natural and weathered feel to the composition.

STYLING YOUR *MYRTUS COMMUNIS*

You will need
- Rake
- Scissors
- Pot
- Mesh
- Wire
- Wire cutters
- Soil
- Scoop
- Rocks

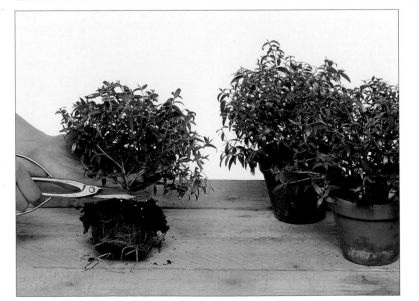

1 Having removed the plants from their pots, rake away the soil to obtain a suitable root-ball and expose the trunk base. Using scissors, remove some of the lower branches to expose the trunk line.

2 Trim each plant into a tree-like form by shortening the long shoots and branches.

3 Prepare the pot in the normal way and add a layer of soil.

4 Arrange some rocks, in this case tufa, so that there is enough space to plant the trees around them, and add extra soil.

5 Place the medium-size tree on the left and settle it into the pot, using a back-and-forth rotating motion so that the plant is bedded well into the soil.

6 Having placed the smallest tree on the right, plant the largest beside it and to the right of the rock. Ensure that this tree is slightly higher than the others. Never finish with the tops of all trees at the same level.

Right: *The final effect should be that of a miniature landscape which has been in existence for many years, so it will be necessary to add various mosses and tiny plants to the surface of the soil.*

Sageretia theezans

Commonly known as the bird plum cherry, *Sageretia theezans* is a popular species for indoor bonsai. Specimens of this plant are normally sold as fully trained trees. This particular specimen has been allowed to grow on and has lost its original shape. The bird plum cherry originates from the Far East where it is often used as a hedging plant, largely because it grows very quickly into medium-sized, shrubby shapes and even small trees. When fully developed, it produces an excellent, textured trunk that thickens very quickly and eventually forms a good, mature, flaking trunk which is especially suitable for bonsai styling.

These trees have delicate leaves which can lose their moisture quickly and dry out. Regular misting of the foliage should control this situation. The roots develop quickly, so repot every year. As the bark matures and flakes away, it will leave a very attractive patchy yellow and orange colouring that is particularly pleasing when the plant has dropped its leaves.

As with many other shrubby plants, the roots of *Sageretia* develop into very compact structures that are ideal for bonsai culture as they will flourish in shallow bonsai pots. This indoor bonsai can also be kept outdoors during frost-free periods of the year, but, because of its very thin, delicate leaves, it can be very vulnerable to many conditions. Strong wind and strong sun – either separately or, even worse, together – can quickly destroy the foliage, so great care should be taken to avoid adverse conditions such as these.

When it is necessary to prune the thick branches or even the trunk of a *Sageretia*, it will soon become very

Above: *This* Sageretia theezans *has been grown in a pot for several years until suitable for pruning and planting in a bonsai pot.*

clear how hard the wood can be. In fact, it may take several smaller cuts to carry out a pruning operation that would need just one cut if you were working with a plant that has much softer wood. For this reason, you will need to make sure that all your pruning tools are extremely sharp, so that the pruning process is made as easy as possible.

STYLING YOUR *SAGERETIA THEEZANS*

You will need
- Rake
- Branch cutters
- Pot
- Mesh
- Wire
- Wire cutters
- Soil
- Scoop
- Chopstick
- Scissors
- Sprayer

1 Having removed the plant from its pot and raked out the roots very carefully, use branch cutters to cut out the central branch which would otherwise spoil the line of the finished tree.

2 Settle the tree into the pot just off centre and fill up with some soil using a scoop. Work the soil into the roots with a chopstick.

3 Using a pair of scissors, cut back the long shoots, leaving just one or two leaves.

4 Mist the soil and plant to create a high humidity. This species has thin leaves that can dry out quickly after repotting, so do this regularly.

Below: *After placing the finished tree in a crackle-glaze pot and shaping it by pruning, press some moss into the soil surface to add a little more realism to the design.*

DISPLAYING BONSAI

When displaying bonsai indoors, remember that they need an airy position in good light, whereas outdoor bonsai require full light and an open situation. Indoors, bonsai are best displayed on some type of display table, perhaps on a suitable mat. Any background used indoors should also complement the tree, being as plain as possible, so that the tree form is not compromised in any way. Outdoors, bonsai can be displayed on specially built stands or benches. It is important that these are high enough for the trees to be viewed at approximately eye-level.

The choice of pot is also important. Indeed, the size, shape, colour and texture of the pot, whether it is glazed or unglazed, and whether it has bold or insignificant feet, are all features that can make or break the appearance of an individual bonsai. None of these elements must dominate the tree, but they must gently complement and frame it.

Left: *A broom-style Chinese elm (*Ulmus parvifolia*) in an indoor situation. Remember to protect furniture from possible damage from water or pot feet.*

Pots and Containers

To the untrained eye, it may seem that the bonsai pot is just the container in which to grow the tree. However, the pot is actually one of the most important parts of the overall effect. The relationship between the pot and the tree is a complex one, and it is most important that the pot blends well with the tree, so that the final composition of tree and pot becomes a complementary and well-balanced single unit. A bonsai in a suitable container can be compared with a classical work of art mounted in a similarly suitable frame. In both cases, your eye should be drawn first by the painting or tree, with the frame or pot later being perceived as the complementary mount. If the reverse is true, then the framing feature will be seen to dominate the intended subject.

Above: *A common beech (*Fagus sylvatica*) in a pot that some might consider too deep, but which works quite well with this tree.*

With bonsai, the pot is the frame, and there should be no conflict over which part of the composition is viewed first. The eye should be drawn first to the lower trunk of the tree, then move up into its apex before considering the pot as framing the whole presentation.

CONSTRUCTION

Bonsai pots will need to be frost-proof if they are going to contain hardy outdoor trees in a temperate climate, and should therefore be made from high-temperature fired stoneware. (Even if trees are to be kept in tropical or subtropical areas, frost-proof pots would be recommended, as they are much tougher.) Pots and containers that are constructed of less sturdy materials, such as mica and plastic, are fine for use by beginners or as temporary training pots, but stoneware pots certainly give the trees a far superior appearance.

Choose pots that have one or more large drainage holes. Larger pots may have a series of small holes around the perimeter of their base; these are for use when you are tying the tree into the pot. The floor of the pot should be flat, so that there are no areas where water can become trapped for any prolonged period.

Make sure that any pots you purchase have good feet. These will raise the base of the pot above the display stand, so allowing free airflow around and under the base of the pot, which will increase the chances of your trees remaining healthy.

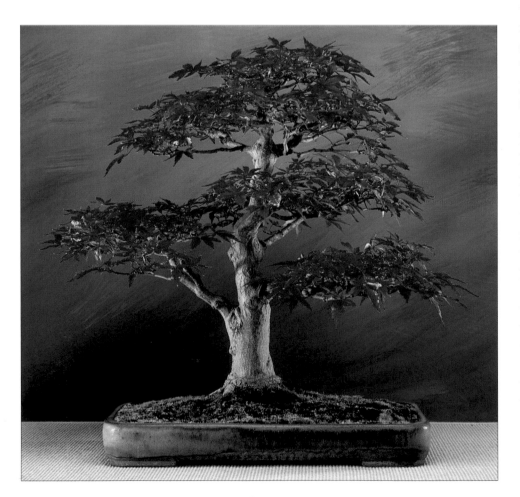

Left: *An informal upright Japanese maple,* Acer palmatum *'Nomura', planted in a suitably coloured and shaped pot.*

STYLES OF POT

Bonsai pots are produced in a huge range of different shapes, sizes and colours designed to suit all styles and species. The accompanying pictures show a small range of available pots. When choosing a pot, it is advisable to take your tree to a pot supplier, who will have a wide range of suitable pots, to make sure that you obtain the best container for your individual tree.

GLAZING

As a general rule when choosing a pot, opt for glazed or semi-glazed pots for deciduous trees and matt (flat) or unglazed pots for conifers and evergreens. Bonsai pots should always be unglazed on the inside, as this will help to keep the tree stable within the pot when the roots have grown sufficiently to come into contact with the pot sides. Any external glazing should run over the rim and a short way down the inside edge of the pot.

Above: *A small ceramic Japanese pot that is good enough to display on its own. Only a small, pretty flowering tree would suit this pot.*

Right: *An unusual cascade bonsai in a pot made by the tree's owner, and exhibited at a Bonsai Kai bonsai competition.*

A RANGE OF POTS AND CONTAINERS

There are some general rules to follow when you are deciding which container is most suitable for a particular bonsai tree. Glazed pots of various colours are much better for displaying broadleaf trees, but remember that they must never be very bright in colour. Instead, the colour should blend beautifully with the shade of the foliage or with the colour of the trunk. Unglazed pots, which are available in varying shades of matt (flat) brown or grey, are much more suitable for conifers and evergreen trees. Outdoor trees, which are more likely to be exposed to frosts, will also require a container that is totally frost-proof.

The container that you choose should also accentuate the form and colour of the bonsai specimen, while at the same time not dominating the tree. Think very carefully before choosing your container, and if you are in any doubt, consult an experienced bonsai artist who will help you to select a pot that complements your bonsai perfectly.

Right: A tall pot such as this is ideal for cascade bonsai because it allows the form of the cascading tree to be seen to advantage.

Japanese slip-cast
lipped rectangle

Japanese slip-cast lipped rectangle

Japanese slip-cast
lipped rectangle

Japanese slip-cast
lipped rectangle

English hand-made
crescent

English hand-made
round

English hand-made
square cascade

English primitive hand-made
shallow round

Chinese decorated
square cascade

English primitive hand-
made shallow crescent

Japanese shallow rectangle

English primitive hand-made
shallow crescent

English primitive
hand-made round

Japanese fluted round slip-cast

English hand-made
rectangle

Japanese slip-cast
lipped rectangle

Japanese slip-cast lipped oval

Japanese shallow
oval

Japanese slip-cast
lipped oval

English hand-made
round

Japanese slip-cast lipped
rectangle

Display Stands

It is very important when displaying any size or style of bonsai to make sure that each element of the display complements the others, as well as the chosen bonsai. This means that the colour and design of any display tables, stands, matting and background should be subtle and blend with the bonsai pot, trunk, foliage and any accent plant involved. Display tables and stands can be purchased from bonsai suppliers or found in stores that sell oriental-style furniture. These accessories will normally be used when displaying any type of bonsai indoors in your own home or at special bonsai exhibitions and shows. All bonsai can be displayed indoors as long as you ensure that outdoor trees are only kept inside for a day or two at the most. As with the pot, the display stand must not dominate the tree.

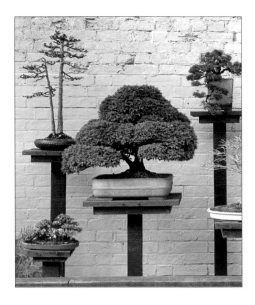

Display tables should always be carefully selected so that they blend well with each individual tree. They are available in a very wide variety of sizes, shapes, designs and colours and are mostly constructed in various types of wood, from oak and rosewood through to ebony or teak – in fact, virtually any wood can be suitable providing it blends with the tree to be displayed. However, good-quality display tables can be difficult to obtain. If you have the ability and skill, and think you can construct your own display tables, then this may be an easier way forward, as you can then custom-build them to your own requirements.

Instead of formal-style display tables, consider using thin slices of good-quality timber as a form of

Above: *This is a typical outdoor display using stands made from pre-treated timber and coloured to taste.*

display. These are probably best suited to displaying groups or forests that are contained in or on a large flat slab or pot. The slice of timber will need to be slightly larger than the slab or pot and be properly finished so that it looks like a quality piece of furniture.

Stand shapes include rectangular, square, round and multi-sided, and range from very low to extremely tall.

Left: *This elegant Chinese elm (*Ulmus parvifolia*) cascade bonsai is being displayed to great effect on a tall Chinese mahogany stand.*

Right: *A modern Chinese tall rosewood stand (left) and an antique Chinese mahogany stand (right), both of which are suitable for cascade-style bonsai.*

Low stands are suitable for most trees, be they formal upright, informal upright, leaning or multi-trunk, while tall stands would normally be used to display cascade or semi-cascade trees, which need the height so that they can cascade down over the side of the stand. The height of the stands depends largely on the overall height of the tree. Again, if you have the facilities, knowledge, skill and ability to produce your own display stands, then you can tailor-make them to suit a specific bonsai.

Above and right: *The photographs here show clearly how important the choice of stand is for your bonsai. Low and tall stands have been used to display the same bonsai, but, because the tree is a cascade, it is much better suited to the tall stand.*

Below: *Clockwise from top right: English oak rectangle; Chinese mahogany round; English oak rectangle; Chinese rectangle (stained softwood).*

Below right: *Rectangular rosewood stand from Taiwan (top) and a Japanese oak rectangular stand from Nihonmatsu City (below).*

Slabs and Rocks

Bonsai are traditionally grown in pots and containers of a certain depth in order to enclose the root structure of each individual tree. However, this is not always the case, because some styles of bonsai can actually benefit from being planted on a thin, flat slab made from stone or slate. If this technique is required, then the bonsai will need to be securely attached to the slab because there are no sides for support as there are with a pot. Suitable slabs can be made of slate, sandstone or, in fact, any type of real rock, because artificial slabs which are made of concrete will almost certainly never look as attractive. Slabs that are made from clay in the same way as pots can be very good and, if made by a good potter, they will look as good as any natural rock.

Ideally, these flat slabs should be formed of a material that is strong enough to take the weight of the individual planting involved. Although the pieces of rock need to be thin for aesthetic reasons, they must not be so thin and weak that they break when they are transported.

Above: *Although this bonsai is in the process of being repotted, it can still be displayed on the slab on which it is resting after repotting.*

There are many types of rock for this purpose, but the best is slate, which is structurally very strong. Sandstone can be very weak when in thin section, so this may not be very suitable, although if a thicker slab were needed, it might be satisfactory.

If you find natural stone slabs hard to find, then a good bonsai potter will make you a slab, provided he or she has a good-sized kiln. You can make an artificial slab using a metal frame covered in glass fibre with a sand-and-cement surface that has been coloured to create the appearance of natural rock.

You might find stone slabs locally, but good bonsai suppliers will be able to advise you. Look out for natural products, such as real sandstone or slate. A visit to a local quarry or stonemason could reveal suitable pieces of stone. As a last resort, you can buy reinforced concrete slabs (the type normally sold as paving), but these are heavy and do not look natural enough.

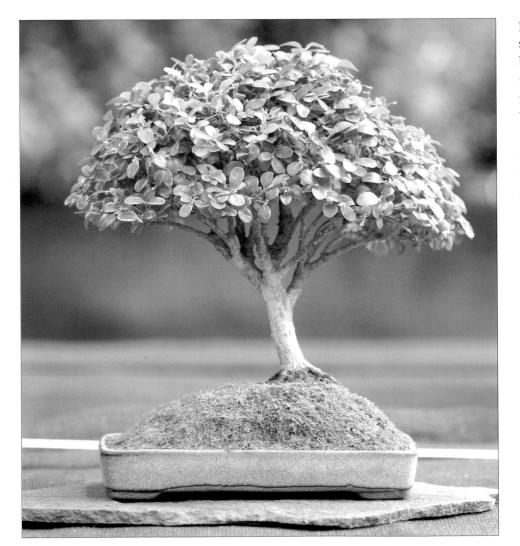

Left: *A "mame" box (*Buxus sempervirens*) displayed on a thin piece of slate. This image was taken at an RHS bonsai show in London.*

SLAB PLANTING A *COTONEASTER* 'CORAL BEAUTY'

1 Select a good-quality specimen of *Cotoneaster* 'Coral Beauty' from a plant nursery.

2 Remove approximately three-quarters of the upper growth and half of the root-ball (roots). Carry out a trial placement of the pruned and styled plant on a sandstone slab.

3 Drill four "tying-in" holes through the slab using a power drill and a masonry drill bit. Always wear safety glasses or goggles when you are using power tools.

4 Pass two pieces of wire through the holes from under the slab.

5 After carrying out initial pruning, place the plant on the slab between the wires.

6 Twist the ends of the two pieces of wire tightly together to secure the tree to the slab. Cut off the spare wire ends.

7 Contour the root-ball by adding a small amount of soil and cover the soil completely with moss in order to create a natural effect.

8 The final arrangement of the bonsai with its slab is pictured here on a suitable surface and against a striking purple background. The tree, soil mound and slab all complement each other beautifully.

Accessories

There are many accessories that can be used with bonsai. These range from stands to labels, and must always complement the bonsai that is on display. Other types of display material, such as bamboo matting, gravel, stone or slate, as well as many other substances, may also be used in the display of bonsai, and you can use a selection of these items to design suitable settings for your bonsai. In all instances, when using accessories such as those already mentioned, consideration must be given to the style, shape, size, colour of both the bonsai and the pot in which it is planted. None of these accessories should clash with or detract the viewer from looking at the bonsai, as it is the bonsai that is always the most important part of each display. That said, all items must be complementary to each other.

Some people like to include all sorts of accessories around their bonsai, but, if too many items are introduced, there could be confusion as to what is the most important item on view, which should always be the bonsai. Therefore, there should never be any item that is not connected with that bonsai, as it will inevitably detract from the appearance of the tree. For example, small figures or figurines incorporated alongside or on the soil of a bonsai are totally inappropriate, as they would catch the eye first and distract the viewer from the beauty of the bonsai.

Above: *This indoor bird plum cherry (*Sageretia theezans*) bonsai has been grown in a glazed pot and displayed on a cut-rush mat.*

MATS
You can use various styles and textures of matting as a base for bonsai as long as they complement, not distract from, the tree itself. You might like to try rush or bamboo matting. Again, it is important to choose matting with a colour and texture that complements the choice of container.

LANTERNS
Stone lanterns can be used in a garden situation where one or, at the most, two (depending upon the size of your garden display area) can be placed strategically alongside some bonsai display stands to give an oriental look to your garden. Any more than two would overdo the situation.

LABELS
Bonsai will benefit from having name labels next to them so that anyone viewing them can instantly identify the species and variety. Any labels should

Left: *Broom-style Japanese grey bark elm (*Zelkova serrata*) on a dark bamboo mat that was chosen to complement the style of pot.*

Left: *Mame-style, informal upright English elm (Ulmus procera), standing on a pale-coloured, thin rush mat. The thin mat complements the small tree.*

Below: *Japanese black pine (Pinus thunbergii) on a piece of mahogany furniture with two accessories that tend to distract the eye from the tree.*

be subtle and the information they display should be kept to a minimum so that the appearance of the bonsai is not compromised.

OTHER DISPLAY ELEMENTS

The time and application that goes into the creation of bonsai trees means that you will want to display them to the best effect. Top-dressings, such as moss and gravel, various fabrics as well as many other substances may well be suitable for use in the display of bonsai. A potted bonsai can be displayed on a thin layer of grit, which can be acquired in many different colours and sizes to suit your tree.

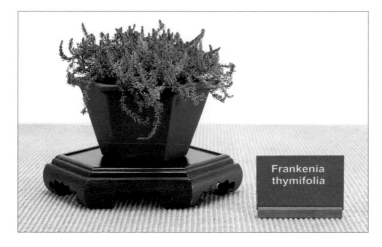

Above: Frankenia thymifolia *accent plant on a hexagonal stand that matches the pot shape. The label is typical of that used at exhibitions.*

Above: *Moss is used as an accessory for decorating the soil surface and is essential for giving a natural look to the completed arrangement.*

Accent Planting

Accent or complementary plants are used to enhance the natural appearance of a bonsai. Full-size trees growing in the wild have various other plants and natural objects around them, including wild flowers, grasses, mosses, lichens and even stones or rocks, some of which may have very interesting shapes. We can draw on these natural features for inspiration when searching for items to display with a bonsai specimen, so creating a more exciting arrangement for the viewer that does not detract attention from the tree itself. Small plants are the most suitable as accents for the majority of displays because their size does not overpower the bonsai. Much larger plants can be used as accents in an outdoor display where they can be used on the ground at the base of a single bonsai display stand.

Suitable material that can be used as accent plants include the dwarf forms of *Equisetum*, *Miscanthus* and *Pennisetum*, as well as *Ophiopogon planiscarpus* 'Nigrescens', *Hakonechloa macra*, *Acorus gramineus*, *Imperata cylindrica*, *Aruncus aethusifolius* and some dwarf forms of *Astilbe*. Many other plants are also suitable for use as accent plants, including daisies, gentians and dandelions, as well as very small bamboos.

In all cases, the accent plants should be potted in complementary containers in just the same way as the bonsai pots complement the trees. When choosing plants as accents for bonsai, it is possible to use plants you have grown in your garden, as well as buying from plant centres. It is easy to develop a blinkered view when deciding on a plant variety as an accent so try to be open-minded and look at any type of small herbaceous or alpine plant. You may be surprised to find that there are many more plants available than you first imagined which would be suitable.

Below: *Korean hornbeam (*Carpinus laxiflora*) with a cyclamen accent plant. Both are displayed on a slice of polished yew wood.*

Above: *Sisyrinchiums make good accent plants. The botanist Theophrastus used the word sisyrinchium for a plant related to the iris.*

Right: *This Japanese black pine (*Pinus thunbergii*) is being displayed with a wild violet accent plant. The rustic accent pot blends well with the rugged trunk of the bonsai.*

SUITABLE ACCENT PLANTS

Above: Frankenia thymifolia *with its russet-coloured foliage is planted here in a deep, hexagonal, matt (flat) brown pot and displayed on a complementary hexagonal rosewood stand.*

Above: Aruncus aethusifolius *growing in a shallow, primitive-style pot. This is a large accent plant and for this reason is more suited to an outdoor display.*

Above: Hakonechloa macra 'Alboaurea' *is quite a large plant with red stems and stripes within the leaves, so the chosen red pot shows off the plant superbly.*

Above: Astilbe × crispa 'Lilliput' *has fern-like leaves and eventually upright stems with pale pink flowers. Again, this is a fairly large plant, planted in this case in a primitive-style pot.*

Above: Ophiopogon planiscarpus 'Nigrescens' *is a very attractive, almost black-leaved plant. The pot is more decorative than normal because it matches well with the curly leaves.*

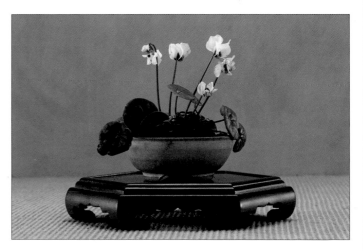

Above: Any small or alpine variety of cyclamen will make a very good accent plant for use with bonsai. Here, a cyclamen is planted in a pot and displayed on a rosewood stand.

Suiseki

These are decorative stones. In traditional Japanese settings, bonsai and *suiseki* are often positioned very close to each other when these two art forms are displayed together. They may, in fact, be regarded as an art form in their own right. Suitable stones can be collected from almost anywhere, such as beaches, river beds, mountain areas, quarries, garden centres and even from your own garden. The main criterion is that each stone must have an interesting shape that can tell a story of its own. Its appearance should also give the impression of a mountain or cliff or other natural features such as these. If the stone has a vein running through it, this might even represent a mountainside with a waterfall or other similar watery outlet.

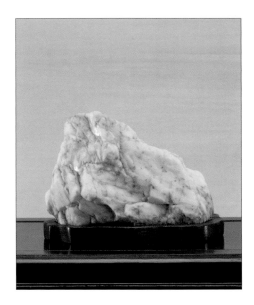

Above: *English Lake District quartz formed into an interesting shape that closely resembles a craggy mountain peak.*

It is thought that the first *penjing* (the original Chinese form of tree and rock landscapes) and *gongshi* (viewing stones) were given to the Empress Regent Suiko of Japan by the Chinese imperial court around AD592–628. These stones were considered to be of great interest to the Japanese aristocracy by virtue of their amazing shapes, which included various features that resembled mountains, caves, waterfalls and many other natural-looking features. They tended to be in the form of stones that emulated the massive, almost vertical, mountains of China. This type of decorative stone became very popular with the Japanese for many hundreds of years.

The Samurai warrior class came to power in Japan in the late Kamakura Period (1183–1333). The teachings of Zen Buddhism became widely accepted by the Samurai as a result of the highly active trading that took place between China and Japan. The disciplines of Zen Buddhism – including austerity, meditation and intuitive insight – meant that apparently simple items in keeping with this philosophy, such as stones with interesting but subtle shapes and colours, were much sought after.

This preference was further emphasized by Zen monks during the Muramachi Period (1338–1573), when the stones were cleaned of all other elements, such as soil, dirt and possibly plant material, thus accentuating their simple but interesting detail.

Over a considerable period of time, stones came to be selected that suggested, by their form, representations of natural landscapes, such as mountains, valleys, caves and waterfalls etc. The Zen monks had a powerful influence over the Japanese ruling class, and these stones were considered to lead to spiritual refinement, enlightenment and inner awareness.

During the Edo Period (1603–1867), the wealthy merchants who came to the fore began to challenge the

Left: *A piece of* ibigawa *rock, displayed here as an accent to an* Acer palmatum *'Kiyohime', which is showing the beautiful branch ramification of its winter form.*

Right: *Californian black jade mountain* suiseki *used as an accent to a* Juniperus chinensis *on an English bonsai stand.*

aristocracy with their interest in *suiseki* and began collecting and competing with them for these stones. During this period, Japan became extremely isolated as a result of closing its borders to all outsiders, but this closure meant that the Japanese arts expanded and flourished without influence from other countries, religions and regimes.

The Meiji period (1868–1912) saw a lull in the interest in *suiseki* largely because of the decrease in wealth of the Samurai and upper classes, but in some ways it began to develop. It was during this period that *suiseki* first came to be classified and given names for certain shapes and styles.

From the middle of the twentieth century, interest in *suiseki* began to regenerate, and it spread into the international arena, as did bonsai. It continues to rise in interest today, so much so that there are now *suiseki* societies, clubs and associations throughout the world.

DIFFERENT *SUISEKI* STONES

Above: *Beautiful slate* suiseki *resembling a mountain with vertical rock faces and sheer drops.*

Above: *Japanese* ibigawa *stone which has many different colours, interesting textures and caves.*

Above: *Coastal rocky island with interesting, water-shaped erosion and textures in a sea of fine white gravel.*

Above: *This Californian jade mountain stone has intriguing caves, waterfalls and sheer rock faces.*

Above: *Another slate* suiseki *with a graduating slope that leads to a dramatic vertical rock face.*

Above: *Very interesting mountain range that culminates in a typically high, imposing alpine peak.*

Indoor Displays

Whatever the climate of your area, and whatever types of tree you have, at some time you will want to display one, some or all of your bonsai indoors. You will need to make sure that the trees you select are in pots suitable for the surroundings in which they are to be displayed. You will also need to take into account the amount of light there is, as well as any direct source of heating, since these aspects may well affect the health of the bonsai in question. With contemporary styling in our homes comes the need to try different ideas when planting and displaying bonsai indoors. Trying different, minimalist containers and placing trees in various rooms can bring a whole new meaning to a bonsai display, but never forget the importance of good light and humidity.

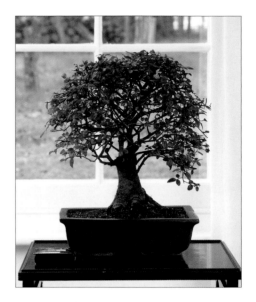

Above: *Broom-style Chinese elm (Ulmus parvifolia) on a table by a north-facing window, a good source of natural light.*

Bonsai should be kept in the correct environmental conditions for the species of plant being grown. Their position also depends on where you live in relation to the natural growing environment of the bonsai that you are growing. They will always need to be in receipt of good natural light, but not placed on a windowsill where the sun can shine directly on to the tree.

It is advisable to place your trees on a table or bench covered with a piece of fabric or any sort of natural material that will enhance the appearance of the tree. The tree can then be placed on a smaller table or mat on top of the fabric. None of these props should detract from the tree in any way: they are simply meant to contribute to the satisfactory display of the tree.

TYPE OF ROOM

A bonsai can be displayed in virtually any room in the home, as long as it is checked regularly to see if it needs watering or feeding and whether the atmospheric conditions are right. Central heating can affect any plant kept indoors, as the conditions will be too warm and dry for successful plant growth. This can be overcome, to some extent, by mist-spraying with water.

The best room for displaying a bonsai is where it can be seen by you and any friends or visitors, such as the sitting room. However, this is not the best room as far as the atmospheric conditions are concerned: a kitchen or bathroom that experiences a certain amount of humidity is preferable.

Tropical and sub-tropical plants may be kept in slightly warm and humid indoor conditions for quite long periods of time, but hardy temperate trees can remain indoors for only a maximum of one or two days before they begin to show signs of stress. If you have to spray the foliage of any tree while it is being displayed indoors, you will need to take care that water droplets do not fall on to polished wood surfaces.

DISPLAY TABLES AND STANDS

The tables upon which bonsai are displayed will need to vary in style depending on the tree. For example, if the tree is powerful and masculine in form, then it will need a stand or table that is strong and powerful, though not so dominant that it detracts from the appearance of the tree. Similarly, if the tree is soft and feminine, then the stand should have similar features so that it complements and does not overpower the tree. The stand should always be complementary to the tree and should never appear to be the main item in the display; nor should it be of a completely opposing colour or design. If the tree has a simple shape, then the stand should be simple. If the tree is more complex, then a more complicated design may be suitable.

Left: *Twisted-trunk Chinese elm (Ulmus parvifolia) displayed in a bathroom which will provide good humidity.*

TRADITIONAL BONSAI DISPLAYS

Traditionally, in Japan, bonsai are displayed in a specially designed area called a *tokonoma* or alcove. It is basically a bench with sides and background within which any object of interest can be displayed. The finished *tokonoma* must have simple, crisp, clean and elegant features. Most people do not have the space at home to construct this type of alcove display, but you may see it at a horticultural show, such as the Chelsea Flower Show, or a major exhibition that deals only with bonsai and related subjects.

In Japan, there are many different shapes and sizes of *tokonoma*, depending on their intended use. Some are used in a teahouse and others for displaying such items as bonsai. The most common version used for bonsai display is called "Kekomi-doko"; it has a wooden floor usually covered with tatami matting and looks like a step up from the surrounding normal floor.

When you are displaying a bonsai in such an alcove or *tokonoma*, it is important that the bonsai is placed on a suitably sympathetic stand or table along with an accent plant, which must also be placed on a suitable stand. In traditional *tokonomas*, there is often a scroll of some description hanging on the back wall. All the items in the display must complement each other. If, however, you are simply displaying a tree for your own enjoyment, then you can place a bonsai on a normal piece of furniture, as long as this does not overpower the appearance of the bonsai specimen.

MODERN BONSAI DISPLAYS

With the advent of more minimalist decor in our interiors, there has been a natural progression into a similarly minimalist style for bonsai planting and displays. So, why not try out some different types of pots, such as glass containers and vases, variously shaped bowls and wooden dishes for displaying your bonsai? These containers can all be displayed on modern pieces of furniture made of any type of material such as glass or various plastics, but remember that good light is required for healthy plant growth. Try standing your bonsai on a shelf in a bathroom, kitchen or sitting room, by all means, but make sure that polished wood surfaces are maintained. If you display your bonsai on an office desk, make sure the light level is high enough.

SINGLE SPECIMENS AND GROUPS

Whether you have only one tree or many, it is worth making the effort to display your bonsai to best advantage. When showing more than one bonsai in a particular place, try to arrange them so that they complement each other, with pots of varying heights and sizes that are suitably positioned.

Above: *Tree of a thousand stars (*Serissa foetida*) standing on a cabinet. Ensure that protection for the polished surface is supplied.*

When displaying several trees in a line, it can be difficult to find a tray for them all, so you may have to find individual trays or dishes for each tree.

BACKDROPS

It is important to use relatively plain backgrounds or backdrops behind bonsai or *penjing* so that you do not detract from the impact of the tree. The tree is always the most important feature and a very busy background may distract the viewer.

Below: *Several trees have been placed indoors on a long, heavy, wooden shelf. The rich, dark colour of the wood provides a good foil for the display.*

Outdoor Displays

Display stands for bonsai kept outside can be very varied and much more rustic in appearance than stands for indoor bonsai. Whatever style of stand you choose, give the trees the dignity they deserve by placing them on good-quality display units. Do not forget the background that will be behind your collection of trees. If they are displayed in your garden in front of a hedge or other trees, you may not even be able to distinguish them. Try to set them against a fence or even a plain painted wall, so that they can be seen in all their glory. When displaying bonsai against a wall or fence, it is also important not to place the trees too close to the background because the tree will "search" for the best light and grow in one direction away from the background. You should also turn your trees regularly to avoid this problem.

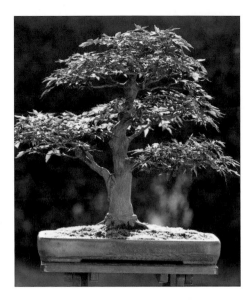

Above: *Medium-sized bonsai, like this purple Japanese maple* (Acer palmatum) *when displayed in front of garden plants can be lost in the busy background, unless it is backlit, as here.*

OUTDOOR BENCHING AND STANDS

Benches made from wood that has been treated with a plant-safe preservative are ideal. They can be supported on wooden stands, legs or even concrete, brick or stone blocks. Reinforced concrete slabs are also suitable if they are available and can be laid across the top of concrete block stands to create a long-lasting display. Remember that most wood has a limited lifespan because it is subjected to all types of weather, so any wooden benches will need to be replaced every 5–10 years, depending on how well they have been maintained.

Strong display benching is very important, and you should make sure that the size and weight of any benching used is suitable for the trees to be displayed. The most suitable height at which to display your bonsai trees is approximately eye-level, so that you can look into the trees from just above the level of the pot rim. Imagine the height from which you would normally view a full-size tree; you will gain the best effect with your bonsai if you can replicate this view, as though you were looking at your trees with the eye of a suitably scaled-down person.

DISPLAYING A LARGE OUTDOOR COLLECTION

If you have a large collection outdoors, then it may not always be possible to provide benching that can be used to display a variety of trees at the correct height. It may, therefore, be a good idea to vary the height of the stands to suit each tree. If you have several large trees, using a table-top that can be rotated will prove to be a considerable advantage because you will need to turn the trees from time to time in order to maintain even growth all round.

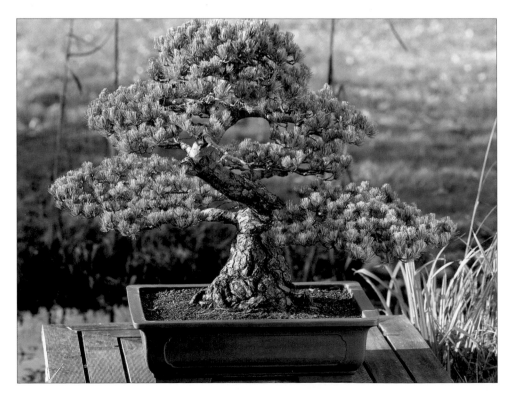

Left: *A large, old Japanese white pine* (Pinus parviflora) *in a garden situation and displayed on wooden decking next to a small pool.*

Above: *Bonsai should be displayed so that their features can be clearly seen. A split-level stand such as this can be used to display trees of different sizes perfectly.*

Below: *European olive* (Olea europaea) *that has been grown as a garden bonsai, although it does not follow the proportional relationship between the plant and the pot, as is customary with traditional bonsai specimens.*

If you have hedges in your garden, then you will need to position your bonsai specimens so that they are far enough away from the hedges to stand out and be clearly seen.

Any background must always be high enough to allow the whole tree to be viewed in front of it and not so short that the top of the fence, wall or hedge simply cuts across the top of the tree.

OTHER POINTS TO CONSIDER

Don't forget that the environmental conditions need to be right for the types of trees your are growing, so think about the amount of sunlight and shelter from wind they will receive. For example, both sides of a wall or fence can be used to provide a background for two different displays.

Many other accessories, such as lanterns and wind chimes, can be included in an outdoor display, as long as they do not distract the viewer from the bonsai.

SUITABLE BACKDROPS

Backgrounds for outdoor bonsai are normally made from natural materials such as wood (usually fencing), stone, or other varieties of plant. Bamboo can be effective, whether growing or cut and made into a screen. A brick or stone wall may be very distracting behind a bonsai, so it is best to paint it with some pale-coloured paint. Should the wall be of an uneven texture, it may also be necessary to render it to achieve a smooth, uninterrupted surface. When the rendered wall is painted, it will provide an excellent solid backdrop, allowing the bonsai trees to stand out so that their forms can be appreciated.

If there needs to be any form of joint in a fence or wall, then it is preferable for these to run vertically, rather than horizontally. Horizontal lines will detract from the appearance of any bonsai because they will "cut through" the form of the tree, whereas vertical lines or joints will accentuate the line of the tree.

Bonsai Shows

Many of the best bonsai are in private collections and are rarely seen by members of the public except when they appear at horticultural shows or special bonsai exhibitions and conventions. It is at these special events that the owners of such collections have the opportunity to display their bonsai when they are looking their very best. Such shows and conventions occur in most parts of the world and it is worth attending one of these events to see top-quality bonsai correctly displayed by very experienced bonsai growers and collectors. Most people who exhibit at bonsai shows and competitions are amateur growers who are members of their local bonsai club or society and who may have been growing bonsai for anything from a few months to many decades.

One of the best-known shows at which you can view bonsai is the Royal Horticultural Society's Chelsea Flower Show. This takes place in late May every year in the grounds of the Royal Hospital in London. At this show there are normally about six bonsai exhibits staged by both professional and amateur bonsai growers, as well as bonsai societies.

Similar gardening shows, take place all over the world and can be a great source of inspiration for visitors, as well as an exciting challenge if you decide to exhibit.

Below: *Part of the author's collection of bonsai at Leonardslee Gardens, West Sussex, England, where the trees are on permanent display on a variety of stands.*

Index

Bird plum cherry (Sageretia theezans)

Ficus benjamina '*Wiandii*'

Acknowledgements

Author's acknowledgements
I would like to thank my wife Ann for her very valuable help with the preparation of materials, proofreading and IT input; Robin and Jane Loder for the use of the facilities provided at Leonardslee Gardens, West Sussex, England; members of Bonsai Kai for allowing photography of their trees; Neil Sutherland for the majority of the photographs and for entering into the spirit of the project.

Publisher's acknowledgements
Most of the photographs in this book were taken by Neil Sutherland. Other images were taken by Peter Anderson, John Freeman and Steve Wooster.

All materials, plants and trees supplied by Ken Norman except where quoted: 77br, 82bl, courtesy **Bonsai Kai**; 78t courtesy **Peter Christian-Lau**. Stands 89cl, 89bc, 89br by **Paul Smith**; 89tr by **Ian Smith**.

Left: You can display an outdoor bonsai indoors for a maximum of a day or two as it cannot tolerate indoor conditions for longer.